Catching The Wave
Of
Workforce Diversity

Powerful New Skills for Managers

Joy Bodzioch, Ph.D.

BookPartners, Inc.

Wilsonville, Oregon

Copyright 1995 by Joy Bodzioch
All rights reserved
Printed in U.S.A.
Library of Congress Catalog 95-80195
ISBN 1-885221-29-0

This book may not be reproduced in whole or in part, by mimeograph or any other means, without permission. For information contact:

BookPartners, Inc.
P. O. Box 922
Wilsonville, Oregon 97070

Dedication

To Adam Bodzioch. You loved, encouraged and believed in me through years of searching. May you now share my joy.

To Greg Bodzioch, Judy Weger, Lynne Stein and the rest of my "family" at the International Churches of Christ. You showed me the only Way to live. May you continue to walk in His love.

To Bill Brandon, John Arnold Smith, Terry Allen and Anthony Williams. You have taught me, toiled with me, tolerated me and at times even tested me. May you experience the deep satisfaction of knowing that, through your passion for and commitment to diversity's most noble values, you are transforming tomorrow's workplace, and thereby transforming tomorrow's world.

To the manager who seeks answers in these pages. You have an awesome responsibility — leading people to fully use their highest abilities. May you be challenged to use these skills in a true spirit of caring, and inspired to study and follow the greatest leader of all time.

Acknowledgements

I wish to personally thank all those who continued to believe in me during my "searching years." Special love and gratitude go to Adam and Greg Bodzioch. Thank you for your patient support — especially during grad school!

Thanks to wonderful "old" Dallas friends, especially Dawn Conklin, Carol Myers, Ellen Pfiffner, Vivian Gardner, George and Jan Clark, Lillian Morris and Cathy Bingman: your encouragement kept me moving forward.

Thanks to nurturing friends in the National Speakers Association, especially Bette Price, Juanell Teague, and the 1993-94 mentee group at the North Texas chapter.

Thanks to all my clients and workshop participants: I've learned from you as you've learned from me! Special thanks to Jenny Peters and Jinger Gibson for your help and encouragement (you became friends, as well)!

Special appreciation goes to all those who have inspired my diversity thinking — especially Michele Ford, John Arnold Smith, Terry Allen, Bill Brandon, Anthony Williams, Pat Cohen-Hadria, author Sondra Thiederman and the editors and contributors of the Managing Diversity Newsletter. Gratitude to James Griffin at KEOM radio, Mesquite Texas, for the opportunity to disseminate my "Diversity Tips."

Finally, being acquainted with publishing horror stories makes me especially grateful to Thorn and Ursula Bacon of BookPartners — your expertise, creativity and patient assistance have made this project a sheer pleasure.

Table of Contents

    Preface 1
1. The Manager in a Multicultural Organization 7
2. Assess Your Team: Using the "Three C's" of Managing Diversity 13
3. Basic Skills for Better Communication with ALL Employees 21
4. Communicating What's Appropriate, Acceptable, and Expected to Diverse Employees 29
5. "Speakeasies": Creating an Environment Where It's Easy To Speak Up 41
6. Understand and Be Understood: Managing Employees Who Speak Limited English 51
7. Coaching Diverse Employees 59
8. Motivating and Empowering Diverse Employees 77
9. Improving Communication Between Men and Women 97
10. Defusing, Managing, and Mediating Intercultural Conflict 107
11. From Different to Exceptional: Creating a Climate for Growing 121
    Appendix 135
        Bibliography and References 135
        Core Values 139
        Sample Role-Play Scenarios 140
        Observer Feedback Sheet for Role-Plays . . .141
        About the Author .143

Preface

What Happened to the "Melting Pot?"

Cultural diversity ... workforce 2000 ... multiculturalism ... reverse discrimination ... the graying of America ... glass ceiling ... gay rights ... the physically challenged ... people of color ... eldercare ... the mommy track ...

Twenty-five years ago these terms were not in our everyday vocabulary. Many of us thought of the United States as a land where everybody is created equal. We were first and foremost Americans! We saw ourselves as a "melting pot" where our differences dissolved so we could "combine" to achieve something great.

But slowly, inexorably, a change was taking place. Transportation and technology were making the world a smaller place. Immigrants and "non-traditional" workers began to press for a voice, for an identity. People began to realize that we never did "melt" very well. Progressive thinkers began to suspect that maybe, just maybe, the strength of America lay in its diversity.

Diversity Opportunities — And Obstacles

At some point, cutting-edge organizations recognized that an increasingly diverse employee and customer base would inevitably present an obstacle to economic and social progress — unless some method could be found to harness and capitalize on ethnic, racial and gender differences. And so was born a new kind of professional: the cultural diversity consultant. Today, diversity training and consulting is big business. In October, 1993, *Training Magazine* reported that 47% of all organizations with 100 or more employees were providing diversity training, up 7% in a single year. According to a May, 1993 issue of *The Atlanta Journal,* diversity consultants in the U.S. at that time numbered between 3000 and 5000. Finally, the American Society for Training and Development estimated that workforce diversity specialists quadrupled between 1990 and 1993.

Despite this phenomenal growth, the diversity field also has been controversial. While each day contributes new names to the list of diversity practitioners, I cannot help but wonder about the qualifications and motives of these new diversity "experts." Published articles have also suggested that, if not properly conducted, diversity training can have unfortunate side effects *(New York Times,* 8/1/93). In the same article, a New Jersey management consultant stated, "I've seen diversity trainers go into companies with wrecking balls and they leave a mess."

Skills And The Bottom Line

Although instances where diversity initiatives caused more problems than they solved are probably rare, a persistent difficulty is that companies typically begin with awareness training and lack the budget (or commitment) to follow this with skill training. A study entitled "Corporate Responses to Diversity" released in October 1994, and reported in the *New York Times* (11/6/94), found that "most of the companies indicate they are doing what is necessary to comply with government employment law and little more. For the most part they have not taken the step beyond what would move diversity out of a pigeon hole in the personnel department and into the strategic center of the corporate environment."

Recent research (Cox, 1993) clearly demonstrates that multicultural organizations can "catch the wave" of the future, capitalizing on their diversity to reap a variety of bottom-line benefits. These include:

- added recruiting opportunities with access to the best available talent
- increased creative problem-solving and innovation
- enhanced service to diverse customers
- lower grievance, lawsuit and turnover costs
- penetration of new domestic and global markets
- improved teamwork and morale
- greater organizational flexibility

At the same time, achieving this goal requires a long-term process of transformation, not simply a one-day session of awareness training. How does this long-term change process begin?

Ideally, top management begins to understand that embracing diversity will result in a more profitable organization. At that point, an external consulting team conducts a cultural audit to identify specific diversity obstacles and opportunities. The resulting data is used to develop a detailed plan for addressing each challenge uncovered during the assessment process.

It is the individual manager, however, who actually drives the change. Why? Because a subtle shift occurs when employees, and especially managers, adopt behavior that recognizes, appreciates and capitalizes on the diversity inherent in the work group. People begin to experience firsthand the benefits of diversity, which then drives further change. The purpose of this handbook is to provide a guide for managers to incorporate effective diversity management skills into their behavior on the job.

What Can You Expect From This Book?

Because the word "diversity" has so many different meanings and connotations nowadays, I believe it is important to state that this book is based on the philosophy that organizations can benefit from meeting the needs of every employee. This means making it possible for every person to be the best he can be. Diversity is about individuality. It's about making more beautiful "music" with an orchestra of very different instruments than we would make with a roomful of trumpets. Most of all, it's about good management and good communication. It is not about targeting certain employee groups, lowering standards or "political correctness."

This book is not intended to replace training or other kinds of diversity initiatives. Ideally, it will provide managers who have previously attended skill training sessions with a quick desk-top reference. The book also is designed as a guide for the manager who may work in a small organization, in which diversity training may be cost-prohibitive, or in which the person with budgetary control does not share the manager's commitment to effective diversity management. For these reasons, each skill is presented in an easy-to-follow format that emphasizes specific how-to steps. Every effort has been made to present necessary information in a clear, concise style, easy to absorb and free of jargon and theories.

The first chapter answers the question, "What new skills are necessary to be an effective manager today?" Each of the successive chapters details a different diversity management skill. Finally, the appendix provides a bibliography of additional resources.

(A book about diversity must be especially inclusive. However, since "she or he" creates an awkward manuscript, I have chosen to use "he" throughout the book as a gesture of cooperation and unity with my male colleagues.)

For additional information about any of the skills included in this book, or to schedule diversity training, please return the form at the back of this book or call 1-800-297-7353.

6 Catching The Wave Of Workforce Diversity

One

The Manager in a Multicultural Organization

Luis has been a manager at a large Southwestern telecommunications company for two years. He is proud of his ability to get along well with every worker on his very diverse team. One of Luis's team members is Anh, a young Vietnamese man who immigrated to the United States six months ago. Anh is an excellent worker: his technical skills are superior and he works many extra hours to get the job done. Since Anh speaks little English, he stays pretty much to himself. Luis may not speak with him for several days at a time.

One day last week, Anh happened to glance up as Luis walked past his work station. Luis smiled and greeted Anh with a cocked thumb and extended forefinger gesture, the typical cowboy "pistol" salute. But Anh was unfamiliar with the friendly gesture; he interpreted Luis's cocked thumb signal as a threat, for the next day he brought a gun to work! Fortunately, a co-worker saw Anh put the gun in his locker and reported it to Luis who, in shock and dismay, *passed the information on to Bill, the director of human resources.*

When Bill confronted Anh, Anh explained that he had brought the gun for self-protection, because his manager, Luis, was planning to kill him! After discussions with both Anh and Luis, Bill concluded that in Anh's culture, hand gestures were often interpreted literally, and Anh had not been in America long enough to understand the cultural differences. Although Luis had taken the company's standard management training course, cultural differences had never been discussed, so he had no idea that Anh might react as he did. The fact that Anh's co-worker accidentally saw the gun was the only thing that averted a potential tragedy. It was concluded that the company might benefit from the services of a diversity consultant.

The Times, They Are A'Changin'

The growing diversity of the United States has become a widely accepted reality. By the year 2000, only about 15% of new workforce entrants will be white male: talented prospective candidates will increasingly come from non-traditional ranks — women, people of color, older individuals, the physically challenged and workers who speak English as a second language. These changes will continue to the point where native-born white males will comprise only about one-third of the total workforce. At the same time, organizations will need 23 million more qualified employees than will be available. Also at issue will be the changed character of external customers. As buyers continue to diversify, the combined spending power of

African Americans, Hispanic Americans and Asian Americans will climb to more than $650 billion by the year 2000. Finally, success in a global marketplace requires the ability to understand and communicate with foreign nationals, both within the U.S. and abroad.

Business leaders are rapidly recognizing that to survive and thrive into the next century they must recruit, retain and develop a non-traditional workforce to better serve a non-traditional consumer market. Although some decision makers have adopted a "wait-and-see" attitude, even the most conservative are persuaded to address diversity issues by recent legislation that increases the ease with which disgruntled employees obtain judgments in discrimination lawsuits.

Is Your Company a 20th Century Organization in a 21st Century World?

Despite the above realities, most companies remain in the dark ages when it comes to management training and employee development. In the typical modern organization, the person in charge of training develops a curriculum to be presented to employees, supervisors and managers. The topics in this curriculum reflect the needs of the organization for critical knowledge and skills, while the content describes the way to apply the knowledge and skills to common business situations. At the heart of most curricula is the assumption that all people are basically the same, and that there is one best way to accomplish a given task.

When most of the workforce in this country consisted of native-born white men, these assumptions worked pretty well. In fact, the assumptions that were made about "the way people are," and about the values and motivations of employees, were taken from observation of native-born white men. There was no great concern with the values, views or motivations of women, people of color or the foreign-born because there were so few of them in the workforce.

Recent research has demonstrated that these assumptions — which have formed the basis of management thinking for the past century — are essentially false. All people are not the same: values and motives differ by gender and they differ across cultures. In short, the same management techniques do not work equally well with various groups, whether these groups differ by age, race, gender, national origin, personality style, religion or a host of other qualities. The bottom line is that there is usually more than one "right way" to accomplish tasks.

Updating Management

Studies show that diverse work groups, properly managed, outperform work groups in which all members are of the same gender and culture. But "properly managed" in the new workforce requires new practices. To continue to be successful, organizations must acknowledge demographic shifts and find ways to enable the new workforce to equal and even exceed former levels of productivity.

Training continues to be an important method of developing employees. And although the training topics are similar to those taught in the past, the content must now reflect the new reality — workforce diversity. Managers and supervisors must learn to "plan, organize, direct and control" in ways which are appropriate and effective with a diverse workforce. Employees must learn to be effective even when their customers and co-workers are different from themselves.

The skills included in this book are intended to update "old management thinking." At first glance, some skills may not appear new; instead, what is changed is the manner in which the skill is applied through the management situation. For example, effective listening is reviewed in Chapter 3. Although traditional management courses have emphasized and taught the basics of listening, I have found that rarely is this skill actually practiced in the workplace. Also, in a multicultural environment, it is critical not only that the manager listen, but that the employee know that he or she is being heard.

By incorporating new skills into your repertoire, you will become a more effective manager. In addition, as you encourage your employees to adopt the methods shown for capitalizing on co-worker differences, they will begin to transform your organization, resulting in greater profitability now and in the 21st century.

12 Catching The Wave Of Workforce Diversity

Two

Assess Your Team: Using the "Three C's" of Managing Diversity

Karen manages a team that recently experienced some interracial conflict. She was relieved to learn that the company had scheduled a half-day of diversity awareness training, which she hoped would resolve the problem. But a week after the training, Karen's administrative assistant Yolanda reported that Gabriella, a Hispanic woman who recently transferred from another plant, had complained that she believed the other team members did not like her because they "all sit together" at lunch and at breaks, and she ends up eating alone. Since Gabriella identified with Yolanda, because she was also a person of color, she wanted to know if Yolanda also had been excluded when she was a new employee. Yolanda told her boss, Karen, that she would invite Gabriella to join her and her friends at lunch, and she thought Karen should be aware of how Gabriella was feeling.

When Karen spoke with Gabriella, Gabriella insisted that she did not want to cause trouble. She said she *guessed she was just feeling left out and missed her old friends at her former plant. Karen realized then that, although recent training had emphasized diversity awareness, skills for more effective relationships had not been explored. Also unanswered was the question whether or not the employees cared about developing a relationship with Gabriella. Karen decided that although the training had been a good start, she would have to follow up by "selling" the team on including everyone, especially new people. Then, somehow, she would have to take an active role in demonstrating skills to the employees for better working relationships. Although Karen knew she was a competent manager, she felt more than a little overwhelmed at the task ahead.*

Discovering Diversity Problems

Purpose: To determine cultural diversity problems inherent in your team or work group, and possibilities for improving teamwork and productivity by resolving these problems. This information will tell you which of the following eight skills you need to use, and in what order.

Importance: To capitalize on the benefits of workforce diversity, your employees must possess three characteristics: a desire to work effectively with those who are different in significant ways, an understanding of personal "blind spots" and potential obstacles to establishing positive relationships, and the ability to handle diversity issues in a sensitive manner. When any of these three elements is missing, a person will be hampered in his efforts to establish positive working relations with diverse co-workers. Although the remainder of this book will concentrate on the third characteristic — the skills necessary to communicate effectively — the manager must prepare his or her team to use these skills by first developing appropriate levels of motivation and knowledge.

Step #1 — Help Your People Care About Each Other.
(Provides willingness, motivation and desire to act effectively.)
Ask yourself:
1. Does each person on my team really want to develop positive working relationships with every other team member? (Do you see evidence that they are really trying to accomplish this?)
If YES, go to the next question.
If NO, meet with your team to discuss the following points:
- Explain that mutual respect is the key to team productivity. (When people respect each other, all members are able to work together for the good of each individual and the group as a whole.)
- Tell them it is your expectation that they will develop positive working relationships with every other team member (which will make the team more cohesive). Invite them to meet with you privately if there are issues or conflicts standing in the way of achieving this goal.

- Get their suggestions for increasing mutual respect. (See Chapter 5 for ideas about encouraging team members to be more open.) Be sure to implement their suggestions or at least explain why these ideas cannot be implemented.
- Be sure to model the kind of behavior you expect from your people.
- If individuals are continuing to create dissension among team members, counsel with them. Refer to Chapter 10 for how to act as a mediator to resolve disputes between employees. Consider a transfer or termination if a person continually refuses to be a team player.

2. Does each person on my team seem to be genuinely interested in encouraging each of the other team members to fully use their abilities?
   If YES go to Step #2.
   If NO:
   - Spend private time with each team member in order to fully evaluate the skills, areas of expertise and positive characteristics he or she brings to the work group.
   - Meet with the team to communicate the unique contribution of each team member to the team as a whole. The purpose of this meeting is to help them appreciate the talents of each other so they can work together more effectively. Be sure to emphasize that the diversity of the team — the different resources each person brings — is the team's greatest strength.

Although caring cannot be legislated, the absence of a caring environment can prevent people from focusing on mutual goals, as the following scenario illustrates.

A large Northeastern utility company hired me to conduct a series of training sessions at each of its locations. The training was piloted at several divisions and received excellent reviews, so the company decided to roll it out to include every employee. Over a period of months, I traveled to a variety of remote locations and, despite the initial resistance of some participants, the evaluations were consistently positive. However, at one particular location, I knew almost immediately that something was amiss. Although the group demographics were similar to other employees I had previously trained, rather than focusing on the planned discussions and exercises, the participants continually made side remarks and jokes, the subject of which remained a mystery despite my efforts to be included.

Some people made sarcastic comments like, "Who is this company trying to fool with this 'valuing diversity' stuff?" When I asked for an explanation, the participants simply laughed and refused to elaborate. By lunch, I was beginning to think I would find another way to earn a living! Fortunately, I was invited to eat with an area manager whose job it was to coordinate the local training. As soon as we were seated, the manager calmly remarked that he wasn't at all surprised at the employees' reaction, and that I shouldn't take it personally.

Then he went on to describe the person who supervised these employees as the "antithesis of diversity values." Not only did this supervisor regularly berate his people in public, he also engaged in behavior that came dangerously close to race discrimination. Personnel had been trying to get rid of him for years, but he had seniority and friends in high places. As the area manager talked, I realized that all the training in the world would not help the man he described, who obviously did not care about his people. When I observed that these employees would never benefit from diversity training as long as they were supervised by a tyrant, the area manager encouraged me to report this perception to the home office, stating that perhaps an outsider would move them to action.

Several months after following up on his suggestion, I checked to find out whether anything had been done. Apparently the information had been passed up the line, and "since the offending employee would probably retire soon anyway," no move had been made to terminate his employment or move him to a non-supervisory position. Without doubt, this decision will have an immeasurable, long-term negative impact on the people and productivity of that particular unit. Like the proverbial "ripple effect," the consequences of such inaction can be far-reaching, negating the positive results of the diversity training and making it appear that the funds for this program were wasted.

Step #2 — Help Your People Develop Awareness Of How Differences Can Impact Relationships.
(Provides understanding of potential barriers to establishing positive relationships.)
Ask Yourself:
1. Is there evidence (conflicts, comments, behavior) that team members underestimate the importance of

age, race, gender, religious or geographic origin differences in determining attitudes, priorities, work-styles or values?
If NO, go to the next question.
If YES:
- Consider scheduling awareness training — preferably one day (at least a half-day) for your team.
- If training is not an option, rent or purchase a diversity videotape, schedule a time for your team to view it, and follow it with discussion. Ask your human resource person to sit in and answer questions following the tape.

2. Does stereotyping occur? Do you catch yourself or other team members making assumptions about people based on their age, race, gender, physical abilities, geographic origin, religion or sexual orientation?
If NO, go to the next question.
If YES:
- Follow the suggestions under question #1.
- Ask for a few examples of stereotypes (e.g., "all Texans wear cowboy boots," "all African-Americans have rhythm," "all women are nurturing"). Make it clear that stereotyping puts limits on people, and so is detrimental to productivity. Encourage team members to catch and challenge stereotypic thinking.

3. Do people engage in behavior that shows a lack of respect for differences? Do they use language (or even laugh at jokes) that shows age, race or sex bias? Are they insensitive to religious celebrations or

holidays? Are they unwilling to be flexible in "covering" for single parents who occasionally must leave work early?
If NO, go to Step #3.
If YES:
- Clearly communicate your expectations to the team, and also the consequences for non-compliance. (See Chapter 4 for suggestions.)
- Model the behavior you expect.
- Ensure that no one is isolated from the rest of the team. Even in informal situations (lunch, for example) people should not feel excluded by the group. Once again, your example is the key — be sure to include people who function on the fringes of the group in discussions and assign them to group projects that will give them opportunities to become better acquainted with other members of the team. Help the team overcome stereotypes that are contributing to exclusion by calling attention to stereotypic thinking and reminding the group that people will be treated as individuals.

Step #3 — Help Your People Develop Communication Skills To Bring Out The Best In Every Team Member.

(Provides the ability to go beyond awareness to act more effectively.)

Ask yourself:

1. Do the people I supervise have a desire for positive relationships and an awareness of cultural differences — but lack the skill to be really effective?

If YES, go to Chapter 3!

Three

Basic Skills for Better Communication with ALL Employees

Suzanne is the controller for a large metropolitan hotel. She sees herself as a strong leader, and she has a reputation of being a no-nonsense, straightforward, efficient worker. Her track record with the company is excellent: she has moved up the corporate ladder in record time, and her employees know exactly what she expects. One of the department's most talented accounting clerks, Lisa, has recently made an uncharacteristic string of errors. She has also seemed distracted and she has come to work late on several occasions. Unfortunately, the department is also in the midst of closing the books, so everyone is working under tremendous time-pressure. But since Lisa is an employee Suzanne does not want to lose, she decides to take a few minutes out of her day to intervene, hoping to prevent Lisa's problems from getting worse.

Suzanne calls Lisa into her office and outlines her concerns. Although she is interrupted twice by emergency phone calls, she manages to explain that although Lisa has been a very valuable employee in the past, her work seems to have deteriorated in recent weeks. Lisa begins to say that she has had some personal problems lately, and apologizes for the errors she has made. At this point, Frank, the data processing manager, bursts into the room, out of breath, and insists that Suzanne is needed at once — otherwise, the department will not make payroll. As Suzanne gets up, she turns to Lisa and says, "I know you'll work it out, Lisa — you know, once you get it together, you'll really have a bright future here!" Then, on Frank's heels she races from the room.

  At the end of the day on Friday afternoon, when Suzanne is finally able to sit down and breathe a sigh of relief, she begins sorting the mail in her in-basket. Opening an envelope with just "Suzanne" written on it, she is dumfounded to discover Lisa's resignation letter. The following Monday, Suzanne receives a call from Bernice, the hotel's director of personnel. Bernice relates the details of Lisa's exit interview: it turns out that Lisa is going through a divorce and has been experiencing child care problems. Because this is a stressful time in her life, she decides to get a job where she hopes to find a "more supportive environment." Suzanne insists, "But I really did everything I possibly could!" Bernice understands Suzanne's position. But she also knows that when managers get too busy or forget to listen, they lose valuable employees. Bernice reflects, "Of course everyone knows they shouldn't bring personal problems to work, but I always feel sad when we lose a good person just because we didn't meet his or her needs." This time, Suzanne is listening.

Building Relationships

Purpose: To create a workplace climate where people feel secure with themselves, connected to other people and able to be accountable for their behavior.

Importance: Before embarking on an effort to capitalize on employee diversity, the manager must possess the basic skills that lie at the root of clear communication — skills for listening to others and expressing personal ideas and feelings. These skills reduce the likelihood of misunderstandings. Although these skills have always been important for managers, they are even more crucial when the manager must communicate with people who possess significantly different attitudes, expectations and values.

Step #1 — Be Sure You Understand Before You Give Advice.
(Builds the relationship and provides useful information for effective problem-solving.)
1. Remember ...
People don't care how much you know
Until they know how much you care!

Advice-giving is probably the single most common barrier to effective listening. When someone has a problem, especially one that sounds familiar, it is only natural to want to help him solve it quickly. But this is not the best course of action! When an employee comes to you with a problem, do you immediately launch into giving advice, or do you really listen to the words, the underlying messages, the employee's feelings? Do you allow the employee to ventilate and get it off his chest even if you can't solve the problem?

2. Play the role of detective.

   Besides letting the employee know that you care enough to listen, avoiding immediate advice-giving gives you time to collect the evidence, ferret out clues to the real roots of the problem, discover whether there are any other witnesses you should talk to before suggesting action, and in general investigate all aspects of the case. As a result, when you do get to the problem-solving phase (which may include advice-giving), you will have a more accurate understanding of the problem and thus be abe to select a workable solution.

3. Begin the meeting with a "specific stroke" — a sincere recognition of one or more of the employee's strengths.

   Whether you are meeting to discuss an employee's concerns, to coach an employee on some new assignment, to review the employee's performance, or even to reprimand someone, it's wise to begin with a sincere statement regarding some positive aspect of the employee's character and its impact on the job. Even with the "problem employee," there is something you can recognize (although you might have to work a little harder to find it). Remember that when positive behavior is noticed and acknowledged, it is more likely to be repeated!

To give a specific stroke, follow these steps:
- Notice a positive attribute (good attendance, punctuality, accuracy, timeliness, neatness).
- Begin with "I" ("I appreciate ...;" "I respect ...;" "I admire ...").
- Identify the attribute ("... your being so patient;" ... your being so hard-working").
- Describe the associated behavior ("I always know I can count on you to be on time;" "The work you turn in is always accurate"). Specific strokes are also great for complimenting the team as a whole. For example, you might begin a meeting by saying, "Before we get to our budget reports, I want you all to know how much I appreciate your being supportive of Mary when she lost her father. The flowers and phone calls really meant a lot to her, and of course that sort of thing makes us a stronger team."

Step #2 — Listen By Practicing "ESR" — Extra-Sensory Reception.

(Goes beyond just hearing, to reading the meaning behind the verbal and non-verbal message.)

1. Ensure privacy: choose a time and place to talk that reduces distractions and interruptions.
2. Begin with an open-ended question (a question that requires more than a yes or no answer). Open-ended questions often begin with "what" or "how." A good opener is "What's going on?"

More examples:
- What can you tell me about it?
- What happened next?
- What did that mean to you?
- How did you understand that?
- How do you know that's what he thought?

3. Ask yourself, "What's he really thinking and feeling?" Play the role of detective (see Step #1, item 2 above.) Watch for gestures or facial expressions that seem to contradict what a person is saying, and ask about these discrepancies (ask, for example, "What did that frown mean?" or "I noticed that you shrugged your shoulders when you said that, almost as if you feel helpless about the situation").
4. Show that you are listening by smiling, maintaining eye contact, leaning forward, nodding your head, and saying "uh huh" to encourage talking.
5. Paraphrase — by restating the content of the message in your own words. ("So it sounds like....")
6. Reflect — by picking up the person's feelings and "mirroring" them back. ("Wow, you sound really angry about that;" "I'll bet you feel pretty frustrated right now;" "I can tell you're really confused about what to do").
7. Summarize every so often by restating your understanding of the speaker's thoughts, feelings and intentions about the situation. ("So it sounds like you felt ... when ..., and you're planning to ....")
8. Ask more open-ended questions as you need additional clarification.

The importance of this kind of listening is illustrated by the following experience.

Several years ago I had a part-time consulting contract with a public-sector educational training organization. Part of my job was evaluating and counseling the students, while the other part was training the staff.

Although it wasn't part of my responsibility, I'd regularly receive calls from staff members who wanted to come to my office just to "talk." I wasn't permitted to allow this to interfere with my regular duties so I often agreed to meet with them at the end of the day. Typically, they were angry at a co-worker or frustrated about something a supervisor had done. Since I had no power to change the situation, all I could do was listen. And while I never spent more than 45 minutes with any one employee, they always insisted that our discussion had been helpful! Unfortunately, these employees didn't feel that their managers had the time, inclination or skills to listen. Had I not been there, I suspect they would have simply swept their concerns under the carpet and continued to do their jobs, with a loss of morale and productivity.

Step #3 — Help Them Solve The Problem — Don't Rescue.
(Assist employees in taking responsibility for their own behavior and help them feel more in control of their lives.)

Once you really understand the employee's concerns and feelings about the situation, it is time to begin problem-solving. This may include some advice-giving, but try the following approach before you launch into giving advice.

1. Ask: "What have you thought about doing at this point?" or "What do you plan to do?" If the employee has a proposed plan of action, ask, "What might happen if you did that — what do you think the consequences would be?" If, after considering the consequences, the employee decides there might be better ways to handle the situation, ask, "What else could you do?"
2. If the employee says "I don't know" or "What do you think I should do?" say, "Since this is a tough problem, maybe we should just think of a variety of options — good ideas, bad ideas, even crazy ideas. That'll get the creative juices flowing! You go first, what's one thing that someone *else* might do in this situation?" (Get a piece of paper to jot down ideas. Take turns and come up with at least 10 different alternatives for solving the problem. Here is where you can give advice by sharing your ideas for a solution. Leave a right-hand column so you will have room to jot down possible consequences later, next to each alternative.)
3. Say, "All right, now let's see what might happen if you did each of the things we listed." Go down the list, asking "What might happen if you ...." Ask this question for each alternative listed. Jot down the most likely consequences beside each option.
4. Once the employee has decided on an alternative for solving the problem, work together to develop a plan of action, including three columns: date, planned action and resources/assistance needed.

Four

Communicating What Is Appropriate, Acceptable and Expected of Diverse Employees

Henry is the sales manager in a mid-size microchip manufacturing company. He is an enthusiastic advocate of managing diversity largely because, as an African-American, he has had to struggle to climb the corporate ladder, and he sincerely appreciated the opportunities given him by a previous employer. He hopes that just as he was empowered to achieve excellence, he can empower the people on his team. There are 28 people in the sales department. Henry believes he has an extremely talented team, and there are positive working relationships among the staff members. Despite the fact that the team includes an almost equal number of men and women, eight people of color, three people who immigrated to the U.S. within the past several years, and two people with physical disabilities, everyone seems to respect each other both personally and professionally.

Henry was shocked when Tamara reported that Bill used a racial "joke" when referring to hoodlums who broke *into a home in his neighborhood. He immediately called Bill into his office for a conference and confronted him with the report, careful not to reveal Tamara's identity. Bill was embarrassed but defended his actions, arguing that he was not referring to anyone in the department by his use of the joke, and that he was only "kidding around." Henry shook his head, unable to comprehend why Bill did not know that his kind of comment would be insulting and unacceptable. That evening, Henry's wife, Shirley, asked about his day at work. When he shared his dilemma, she remarked, "I guess you can't take anything for granted!"*

Establishing Ground Rules

Purpose: To establish "ground rules" for communication in the work group, as well as the consequences for violating these expectations.

Importance: In a diverse workplace the manager must take the lead in clarifying his or her vision of the ways employees will, and will not, communicate with each other, and the benefits of clear and respectful communication. In the absence of these ground rules, employees tend to fall back on old patterns of interacting, which include sweeping uncomfortable feelings "under the rug," using humor that is tinged with racial or sexual innuendo, gossip and sarcasm, and running to the manager with complaints or conflicts that could be resolved by the employees themselves. There is no reason why a multicultural workplace cannot include the same level of camaraderie present in more traditional settings. However, when "fun" happens at the expense of certain employees, it creates an environment that is detrimental to morale and, in the long run, damages teamwork and productivity.

Step #1 — Describe, In Writing, What The Team Needs To Accomplish, The Desired Kinds Of Relationships Between Members Of The Team And Specific Employee Actions That Will Make This Vision A Reality.
(Clarifies what you plan to achieve in your own mind, in preparation for communicating your expectations to the people you supervise.)
1. Spend some quiet time answering the following questions in writing:
   - In a perfect world, with perfect employees, what would the relationships between people be like in the perfect work group? Specifically, how would people act toward each other in order to relate this way? (Focus on how this would be different from the norm.)
   - In a perfect world, with perfect employees, what would my work group be able to achieve? How would the kinds of employee relationships described above make possible this level of achievement?
   - Going back to the first item above, what kinds of relationships can I reasonably expect from the employees in my department?

- How will people need to act toward each other in order to accomplish this?
- What will these relationships enable us to achieve and why?
- What will be the consequences for breaking the ground rules? (Be specific and be sure to include only consequences that you're willing and able to enforce! Consider a warning system such as "three strikes and you're out." Also, be sure that your system of consequences is consistent with company policy.)

2. Develop ground rules to prevent or resolve situations that have caused conflict or negative feelings in the past. Consider including the following:
   - No labeling or name-calling (based on age, race, gender, geographic origin, sexual orientation, etc.)
   - Every person is valued and respected for his abilities. (We will emphasize the contribution each employee can make, regardless of whether we agree with or approve of his lifestyle.)
   - Every person will be expected and assisted (by all other employees) to succeed and do his best.
   - Employees are expected to work toward resolving differences on their own before requesting the manager's intervention. (Step #3 below describes a suggested procedure for resolving co-worker disputes.)

Step #2 — Meet With The Team To Communicate Your Expectations.

(Gives your team members the benefit of sharing

your vision, knowing in advance how the team can accomplish that vision, understanding their personal role in contributing to the realization of this goal and the consequences to expect if they refuse to take the expected actions.)

1. Begin by telling the team that you strongly believe that having a group of diverse employees — in age, race, gender, cultural background, religion, geographic origin (choose the dimensions that apply to your group) — can be a significant advantage. This is because diverse employees bring different strengths, skills, areas of expertise, ideas and perspectives, which have been shown to increase team innovation and productivity. But the team can only reap these rewards if each team member feels valued and respected, and if team members communicate constructively. As a result, you want to share some specific guidelines, or ground rules, for how you expect people to communicate with each other. You also want them to ask questions about any of these that are not clear, and feel free to suggest other ground rules they think should be added to the list.

2. Hand out a working copy of the ground rules you have developed for the team. Discuss each item, one at a time, and ask members of the group to give examples of specific situations that would be covered by that ground rule. (E.g., if the ground rule is "no labeling," an example would be that it is not okay for men to call women "broads." If the ground rule is "respect people for their real abilities," it is not acceptable to assume that a person in a wheel-

chair cannot give a presentation or that a woman should plan the food for a party since "women are better cooks.")

Next, ask what other rules might be added to the list. Invite the team to share new items to be added to the list either now or at any future staff meeting. Also, encourage team members to ask for clarification at any time regarding any of the items, and to discuss difficulties in putting the ground rules into practice.

Finally, discuss the consequences for violating these ground rules.

Encourage team members to catch each other following (or violating) the rules and provide appropriate feedback. Let them know you expect them to report repeated violations to you.

Once the group understands and agrees upon these ground rules, have have them printed in large type and distributed to every team member for posting in work areas.

The longer I do this type of work, the more I am convinced that the term "offensive behavior" has very different meanings for different people. A manager recently told me that a female employee complained about "sexually-explicit material," which had been left on the computer terminal that she inherited when another employee left the company. When the manager investigated, this so called "sexual" material included photos of women in very conservative swimsuits. I myself have been accused of using terminology that insults members of my audiences. One especially memorable experience involved my having commented that I felt "fat," after which a large woman approached me and said that I should have more respect for overweight people. Although we might think that these people were overreacting, we can never judge that their perceptions were wrong.

To each of us, our perceptions are reality. Consider my African-American colleague who went to England, where black people are routinely called "coloured people." She was surprised but not insulted — would you be? We can learn a valuable lesson here. Although there are some behaviors that are unquestionably offensive, many others fall in that "gray area" — offensive to some people but not to others. No matter how we try to be aware of the sensibilities of others, we will occasionally fail. But if we genuinely respect each other, we can forgive an unintentional mistake — and tactfully teach each other how we want to be treated.

Step #3 — Teach Team Members To Resolve Conflicts On Their Own.

(Encourages responsibility and accountability; builds problem-solving and leadership skills; frees you up to handle top-priority projects.)

1. Share the following conflict-resolution procedure with the team members. When differences arise between team members, they are expected to take responsibility for acting as follows:
   - The parties agree to meet at a mutually-convenient time and location. Once together, they

decide who will go first (usually, the person who is most directly affected by the problem).
- Person #1 begins by expressing his or her viewpoint while person #2 listens and paraphrases. (Refer to Chapter Three for more information about effective listening.) It is essential that person #2 refrain from responding, explaining, justifying his actions or suggesting solutions at this point. Just listen — paraphrase thoughts, mirror feelings and ask questions for clarification. Make a sincere attempt to understand the other person's experience, summarizing every so often to verify your understanding of what he is saying. Encourage team members to put themselves in the other person's shoes and imagine how they would feel in similar circumstances. Person #2 can jot down important points or questions as the other person talks, but this should be done quickly to maintain eye contact. (Remember that there are cultural differences in eye contact. Refer to the Appendix — see Thiederman, S.)
- Person #2 now expresses his or her viewpoint and person #1 listens. Once again, person #1 must avoid the temptation to explain or try to solve the problem.
- When both people have fully explained their positions, they work together to brainstorm and list as many possible alternative solutions to the problem as possible. The key here is to agree on something they both want to get from the situation

and then find a way that either they both win or compromise is possible — one person gives in one area, while the other person gives in another area. (At the very least, they can agree that they want to get their conflict resolved so they can work together, reduce the distractions caused by the dispute, and prevent future similar problems.)
- If able to agree, they select a solution. Then they document the meeting by sending a brief description of the dispute to the manager along with the alternatives discussed and the resolution.
- If no resolution is reached, the manager then meets with them to serve as a mediator. (Note: smart managers strongly encourage team members to work these situations out without the manager's direct intervention. Make it clear that it is to their credit if they are able to resolve the problem on their own.)

2. If at all possible, take time for team members to role-play the above steps, using hypothetical problem situations. (Call on your training manager or HR person if you feel you need some additional coaching on effective listening and problem-solving skills.) A good way to conduct this role play is to break the team into small groups of three persons each. Begin by giving each small group three different scenarios and six copies of an observer feedback sheet. The Appendix contains sample role-play scenarios and an observer feedback sheet. Or, write your own scenarios based on problems that have come up in the past, but change the situations

enough to maintain confidentiality. Also, give each team member a copy of the six problem-solving steps listed under item #1.

One person begins by reading the scenario aloud so everyone knows a little about the situation. Of course, the employees will need to be creative to fill in the details. The actual role play now begins. Person #1 explains his or her viewpoint while person #2 listens and person #3 acts as observer. While person #1 is talking, the observer rates how well person #2 is listening (the observer should write person #2's name at the top of the observer feedback form). After person #1 finishes, the observer writes person #1's name at the top of a second feedback form. Now person #2 talks and the observer rates person #1 on his or her ability to listen. When both people have finished talking, the observer discusses how effectively each person listened to the other, and gives each written form to the appropriate person. Then, using a different scenario, persons #2 and #3 resolve a dispute while person #1 is observer. Finally, with a third scenario, persons #1 and #3 resolve a dispute and person #2 acts as observer. In this way, each person has an opportunity to act as observer, and each person has two opportunities to practice listening and problem-solving. Note that the observer does not become involved in the discussion: his or her sole purpose is to assess the listener's skill and provide feedback after the role play.

To save time, you may choose to have the groups

go through all the problem-solving steps on the first scenario, but then stop after the third step on the second and third role plays. But be sure to expose employees to the entire sequence of steps at least once. You will also notice that this process has another advantage: it gives each team member practice in becoming a more effective listener. (Refer to Chapter Ten for more information about conflict management.)

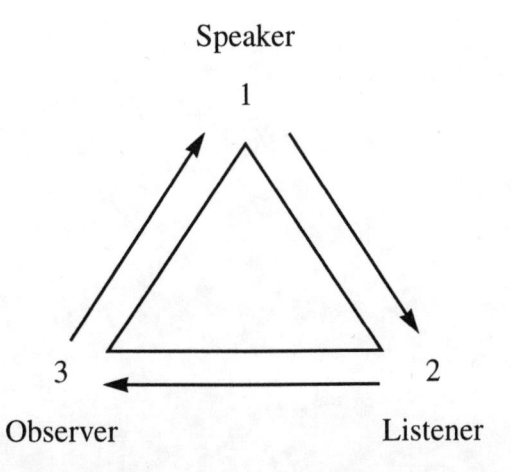

Speaker
1

3 — Observer   2 — Listener

(Following each scenario, rotate after both parties have spoken. Thus, everyone plays all three roles.)

Five

"Speakeasies": Creating an Environment Where It's Easy To Speak Up

Jason manages the quality control section of a computer software company. He has been receiving customer complaints on a particular program, so he decided to call a staff meeting to set up a protocol for resolving the problem. In his usual, organized style, Jason spent the evening before the meeting preparing a protocol. That way, he reasoned, the meeting could proceed quickly and people would not have to take valuable time away from their jobs. Just as he had hoped, he was able to present his plan within 30 minutes. Before the staff left, he asked whether anyone had anything to add. Marva, an older woman with a tendency to talk a lot, said she thought that parts of the plan should be assigned to different people in the department. Then she went on to explain how her version of the plan might work. Jason finally interjected that he really felt the original plan would be most efficient. He asked, "Does everyone agree?" and since there were no further comments, he adjourned the meeting.

Two weeks later, when the team met again for a follow-up, he was amazed to discover that not only did people now have serious reservations about the plan, but the department had fallen significantly behind schedule because of an obvious lack of commitment to carry it out. In frustration, Jason stormed out of the room saying, "Then you solve the problem!"

Where did Jason go wrong? In his unwillingness to really listen and his hurry to end the meeting, he failed to be certain that, in fact, his team members were agreed and committed to his plan of action. Had he explained why he preferred his plan and then followed his comments with an open question like, "What do you think?" he would have quickly learned of the group's reservations. The old saying, "Haste makes waste" certainly applies to business communications!

Create An Open Atmosphere

Purpose: To create an atmosphere of openness that encourages employee involvement.

Importance: A positive aspect of workforce diversity involves the additional ideas, perspectives and skills that diverse employees bring to the workplace. Numerous studies have demonstrated that although diverse teams may take more time and effort to establish positive interpersonal relationships, in the long term they tend to be more innovative and more effective at solving problems than homogeneous teams. However, to enjoy these benefits there must be an expectation and an opportunity for employees to speak out. This chapter will describe a 3-step process for creating the kind of environment in which people are not afraid to share their creative ideas, their different ways of approaching problems and even their disagreements. In some circumstances (e.g., in a crisis where rapid responses are crucial), it may not be feasible or even beneficial to invite employees to collaborate. But, most of the time, the advantages of employee involvement far outweigh the disadvantages.

Step #1 — Ask For Input.
  (Opens the door for openness to occur.)
  1. As much as possible, ask open-ended questions. (Chapter 3, step #2 presents instructions and examples of open-ended questions.)
  2. Ask questions even when you expect a negative response. Notice and comment on non-verbal behavior that suggests that the other person has a concern. For example, the other person may look bored or distracted, be frowning or fidgeting or have a "show me" expression. Although it is human nature to want to avoid disagreement or confrontation, effective communicators will turn these situations into opportunities for openness. Sweeping negative perceptions or feelings under the rug often results in employees who sabotage results or whose low morale poisons the rest of the group.
     An effective way to begin is by describing the

behavior you are observing. For example, you might say, "You seem to have a puzzled look. What are you thinking?" or "I noticed that you just shrugged your shoulders. What did that mean?"

Keep in mind that other cultural groups attribute very different meanings to non-verbal behavior. Among many women in the U.S. and in some Asian cultures, for example, nodding the head means, "I hear you," or "I understand," not "I agree"! Also, some of our common hand gestures in the United States are X-rated in other countries. (Refer to S. Thiederman in the Appendix for further information on differences in non-verbal communication.) Of course, no one can be expert in all cultural traditions.

If you genuinely care and sincerely attempt to understand the people you manage, they will not only forgive the occasional mistake, but will educate you in a spirit of cooperation and good humor.

3. Wait for an answer! Although this seems obvious, we have all had the experience of attending a meeting where the leader asked, "Any other suggestions?" and then immediately added, "Okay, see you next week!" When we are hurried or are not really interested in considering negative feedback, we unintentionally leave the impression that we do not want employee input.

The importance of asking and waiting for information is illustrated by the following experience.

Several years ago I was asked to design and

implement a social skills training program in a large Job Corps center. Part of my responsibilities involved training the staff members in using the skills, so that they could then model them to the Job Corps students in the classroom. On one particular day, I faced an especially challenging group of instructors. They obviously were there against their will. Some of them appeared to be sleeping as I doggedly reviewed the skills. There was very little discussion. As they left I glanced at the evaluation forms for the training session. They were terrible! Over the next two weeks, that group of instructors began to sabotage our efforts by telling some of the students that these skills were not important — "just concentrate on your regular classes and you'll be fine." I decided to take action, although I did not look forward to facing those instructors again.

When they arrived I said, "Look, I know you're angry, but I don't know why. Tell me what's going on and maybe we can work something out." No one said anything — that was the longest pause I've ever experienced! Finally, someone spoke up, and then someone else, and then it seemed they were all talking at once. They said yes, they were angry! Their schedules were already too full, they were up against tight deadlines on their regular work, they were feeling unsupported and they did not need another set of skills to teach!

I said something inspired like, "Wow!" And then something interesting happened. Having gotten it off their chests, they began to suggest a variety of ways to improve the social skills program. Over the next few weeks we implemented most of those suggestions. Not only did their ideas contribute to the eventual success of the program, but this particularly resistant group of instructors became the most vocal advocates of the program. I learned first-hand the value of asking for input — and waiting until I got it!

Step #2 — Accept What They Say, Even When You Don't Agree.
(Provides evidence that you practice what you preach, and thus reinforces the perception that you are truly interested in employee involvement.)
1. Treat employees with unconditional, positive regard. What does this mean? Here is an experience that may answer this question. Recently, on a flight from California to North Carolina, the seat next to me was occupied by a person of the Buddhist faith. Although we certainly did not agree (and perhaps did not even approve of each other's lifestyle), we were able to listen and learn from each other. Unconditional, positive regard communicates that "you are a human being and are therefore valuable and worthy of respect." Even when an employee makes a statement that is completely off-base, an effective manager can really listen, ask questions to clarify (and maybe determine the source of the misperception) and paraphrase or respond honestly with, "That's an interesting way to look at it."

In other words, practice those listening skills. You will notice that this point comes up often, but the importance of listening cannot be over-emphasized. Think about it — professional counselors get paid hefty fees — for what? To listen! When someone really tunes in to us, we feel accepted, which then

increases our self-esteem and ability to take constructive action. (Refer to Chapter 3 for listening tips.)
2. Think about someone you really trust, someone with whom you could share your deepest, darkest secret and he or she would still accept you. Now consider this question: What does that person do to make you feel accepted? When we ask this question in workshops, we usually hear things like, "They keep things private" (confidentiality); "They share their secrets too!" (mutuality); "They're really interested in me and not just themselves" (caring enough to understand).
3. If necessary, agree to disagree! Sometimes we feel we have an obligation to educate people — to convince them that they should agree with us. In some situations, though, it's not possible to change a person's mind. A basic philosophy of diversity is that people have a right to their own perceptions. Can you value the person even when his opinion differs from yours?

Step #3 — Act On Suggestions — Don't Be Afraid To Change.

(Convinces employees that you are willing to be humble — to admit that you may have been wrong, or that they may know more than you do about something. By so doing, you provide an effective model of change for your people.)

1. Embracing diversity is not just about about learning how not to offend other people. It is also about encouraging them to take action by letting us know,

in constructive ways, when they are offended. Let's say I offend you (unintentionally, of course!) It is your responsibility to let me know that you were offended — and do so in a way that increases the likelihood that I will hear (and heed) your feedback. You might say, "I know you probably didn't mean anything by it, but I felt offended when you ... because .... In the future, I'd really appreciate it if you'd....." Notice, in this example, how you (the offended person) have given me the benefit of the doubt ("I know you probably didn't mean anything by it"). Also notice that, instead of accusing me of being an obnoxious louse, you used an "I" statement to express your feelings ("I felt offended when ...").

2. Now it is my responsibility to act on the information you have just provided. Although I may not admit that I've offended you intentionally, and I may not even understand why my behavior would be offensive to you — in fact, your perception may seem totally unreasonable to me — I must agree that to you, your perception is reality. For this reason and because I want to build a positive relationship, I will change my behavior to conform to your wishes.

3. Sometimes managers receive employee suggestions anonymously — for example, in a suggestion box. It is extremely important that these suggestions not be taken lightly, since some employees feel strongly about certain issues but are uncomfortable voicing their opinions personally. How managers respond to items in a suggestion box can have a tremendous impact on employee morale. At the very least,

managers need to thank the team for providing suggestions, and explain to the group why a certain suggestion cannot be implemented. Obviously, a more positive outcome is that the employee's suggestion actually be followed (or perhaps a variation of the suggestion), and if the employee is willing to reveal his identity, he can be given credit for making the suggestion.

Six

Understand and Be Understood: Managing Employees Who Speak Limited English

Adam is the plant manager for a large tool and die manufacturer. Due to a recent increase in Korean and Southeast Asian immigration to the area, the employee population has become largely Asian. One of Adam's recent hires is Phun, a Cambodian man with strong technical skills but limited fluency in English. Last week Adam showed Phun how to use a new piece of equipment. Throughout Adam's explanation, Phun said, "Yes, yes." Then Adam asked Phun if he understood, and again Phun responded with, "Yes!" Today, Adam realized that apparently Phun had not understood at all. Last night Phun failed to turn off a critical power switch, and the motor burned out. Not only will the repair be costly, but since the machine is crucial to the manufacture of the plant's primary product, schedules will be delayed and profits lost.

Adam decides to consult with Huong, another Cambodian man who has worked at the plant for several years. Huong explains that, to Phun, "Yes" means, "I hear you," not necessarily, "I understand." Also, Huong guesses that Phun might pretend that he understands to save face. As Huong leaves the office, Adam just shakes his head in bewilderment. He remembers a time when communication was much easier!

Overcoming Language Barriers

Purpose: To communicate more effectively with those whose primary language is not English.

Importance: As foreign-born people continue to immigrate to the U.S., and companies increasingly focus on the global marketplace, every manager will require skills that ease communication with those who speak limited English. Even when employees take responsibility for learning English, the manager must ensure that language barriers do not hamper communication in the work group or prevent talented foreign-born people from making a contribution. This chapter includes three specific skills: understanding the foreign-born speaker, increasing the likelihood that you will be understood and determining whether in fact you have gotten your point across. Notice that many of the suggestions listed below can also be used to improve communication with anyone on your team!

Step #1 — Improve Your Ability To Understand The Person Who Speaks Limited English.

(Increases understanding of non-native speakers, especially while they are new employees and you are growing accustomed to their accent.)

1. Don't rush — take time to communicate. If you slow down, you will encourage them to do the same. The pressure to speak quickly can often make a person much more difficult to understand.
2. Paraphrase and summarize often. Repeat in your own words what you think you are hearing. For example: "Let me see if I understand. You're saying that.... Is that right?"
3. Encourage written communication. Let the employee know that you consider his ideas very important and ask him to send you a brief memo summarizing his main points, especially following a telephone conversation (since telephone calls lack the visual feedback of face-to-face communication). Or, send *him* a memo to confirm the discussion. Sometimes there will be certain words that are especially difficult for him to pronounce; have paper and pencil handy and encourage him to write them out. Also encourage him to use visual aids like diagrams as he talks.
4. Pay close attention to body language. Although non-verbal signals can mean very different things to non-native speakers, you can still pick up a lot of information this way. You can even learn to read the employee's lips with a little practice. And do not forget to confirm your understanding with the employee before you assume that you are completely accurate.

5. If necessary, use another employee as an interpreter for the first few meetings until you get used to the accent.
6. Try to learn some words in the employee's native language. This communicates that "We're both learning" and encourages a sense of humor about your struggles to understand each other.

Step #2 — Increase Your Listener's Ability To Understand. (Reduces the likelihood of a misunderstanding when you are directing employees.)

1. Avoid shouting and the use of slang and jargon. Many of our most commonly-used words and expressions are slang. The literal translation of the words usually has a very different meaning from the slang expression. For example, if you said, "I know you put a lot of elbow grease into that project," a foreign worker might deny that he ever had a jar of elbow grease! Other examples are the terms "spell it out," "take charge," "put your mind at rest," "take heart," and "throw in the towel." The next time you are communicating with a person who is just learning English, try to catch yourself when you use expressions like these, and restate your message in different words. (This can even be a problem in different parts of the U.S. My friend from Texas recently ordered a hamburger when he visited New York. He told the cook to "cut the onions" — which in Texas means "no onions." He was later shocked to discover that there were chopped onions on his hamburger!)
2. Speak slowly and distinctly, and use short, simple

sentences. Have you ever tried to watch a foreign-language television show? Even if you have some knowledge of the language, you will understand almost nothing because of the speed at which people talk and the complexity of their sentences. Remember to speak concisely, slowly and enunciate clearly. This does not mean you should sound like a robot — just take your time and repeat important ideas in several different ways. Say, "In other words …"

3. Use visual aids, such as diagrams, job aids or handouts to illustrate your main points.
4. Frequently check for understanding. Although it is a good idea to ask workers if they understand, keep in mind that some employees are embarrassed to admit that they are confused. A better approach, especially when it is essential that the employee understand, is to ask *him* to repeat back what you have said. Say, "I'm not sure I've been very clear. How about telling me in your own words what you're going to do on that project?" By accepting responsibility for making yourself clear you take the pressure off the employee and communicate that "We're in this together."
5. If necessary, you can ask a bilingual employee to assist you as interpreter. Of course, the more you "bite the bullet" (another good example of slang!) and communicate with non-native speakers, the more quickly they will learn English and the more quickly you will develop a productive working relationship.

Step #3 — Determine Whether You Have Been Understood. (Helps you evaluate whether you've gotten your points across.)
1. Be alert for signals that the employee does not understand. Examples might be blank looks, frowns, fidgeting, self-conscious laughter, looking away or efforts to change the subject.
2. Sometimes "no questions" means "no understanding." Instead of saying, "Do you have any questions?" ask the open-ended "What questions do you have?"
3. Avoid asking, "Okay?" after giving directions. Often, non-native speakers will say "Yes" to mean "Yes ,I hear you," not "Yes, I understand." Instead, ask the employee for questions, and then thank him and tell him you will be checking back with him later. The best way to find out whether he has understood is to observe his behavior to see if he follows your directions.

Should employees be required to speak English? Read the following scenario before you decide.

A manager at a company with a large population of foreign-born employees recently told me they have a new rule: employees must speak only English in the workplace. Aside from the fact that this will certainly be a very difficult rule to enforce, I wonder whether this decision was carefully considered, and what the impact will be on their long-term morale and productivity.

Speaking English in the workplace is an issue that regularly comes up in our consulting and training activities.

Understand and Be Understood: Managing Employees Who Speak Limited English

Employees whose native language is English say, "Don't they know it's rude to speak their own language when I'm around?" Typically, these employees are convinced that the non-English speaking employees are "talking behind their backs." When we're fortunate to have the perpetrators in the training room, we often ask them why they sometimes prefer to speak their own language. They always explain that they do not want to lose the ability to speak their language, that when they are under a tight deadline it is more efficient and less stressful to speak their native tongue, and that speaking their own language helps them maintain their identity and heritage.

Obviously, there are times when employees must speak English so everyone understands what is being said. But in an environment where people really want to communicate, the limited-English speaker will be sensitive to the feelings of the native-English employee, and the native-English employee will feel comfortable asking colleagues to speak English or to translate if they are feeling left out. Attempts to legislate a positive work environment are likely to backfire by creating the perception that speaking multiple languages is not a valued skill, and by encouraging employees to be devious when communicating with other people from their native lands.

Seven

Coaching Diverse Employees

Lee is a manager in a public sector natural resource management firm. Today he plans to have a conference with Charlie, a Chinese-American employee who has been a member of his team for three years. Lee is really looking forward to this meeting — not only does he like Charlie, but he is excited about offering Charlie a promotion. Lee notices that, as usual, Charlie is early for his appointment. Lee smiles to himself, thinking, "That's just one of the things that makes Charlie such a great employee." Lee greets Charlie with, "Good morning, Mr. Charlie Wong," as he opens the door of his office. In his typical pleasant way, Charlie responds, "And good morning to you, Mr. Lee Bailey!" Once Charlie is seated, Lee asks how Charlie is doing and whether he has enjoyed his parents' visit from China. Charlie answers that his parents returned to China last night, and that although he and his wife enjoyed the visit, his wife will be happy to have a quiet house again. Laughing, Lee agrees, commenting that his wife felt the same after her mother visited at Christmas. Lee moves to the purpose of the meeting:

Lee: "You've worked here three years now, and you've been an excellent employee. You're always willing to do what's necessary to get the job done — even when it means putting in extra hours. Your work is always accurate and you're much faster to learn new things than the others on our team."

Charlie: "Oh, it is nothing."

Lee: "And you also get along well with the others. I'm sure they all respect you!"

Charlie: "Well, (looking embarrassed), I just do my job."

Lee: "But I want you to know how much I appreciate your hard work. And I also think you're ready to become our new group leader!"

Charlie: "No — I'm sure there is someone better to be group leader."

Lee: "But I'll help you learn! And it will mean a pay raise too!"

Charlie: "I am just a hard worker. There are many of us. Maybe Mike would be group leader."

Lee: "No, I'm sure you're the man for the job. I thought you'd be honored!"

Charlie: "I am honored you have thought so highly of me. But I am sure there is someone better."

Lee: "All right, if you insist, we'll discuss this later. But please consider it — you deserve this promotion, and I know you'll be successful!"

As Charlie leaves, Lee closes the door. Sinking into his chair, exhausted, and resting his head on the chair back, he gazes absently at the ceiling. "Why won't Charlie accept *this promotion?"*

Unfortunately, Lee does not understand that people from Charlie's culture often value group harmony more strongly than they value personal advancement. Likewise, they often believe that calling attention to oneself (for example, by accepting a promotion) will disrupt this fragile harmony. Once armed with this information, Lee might be able to persuade Charlie by explaining that Charlie's acceptance of the position will help Lee save face, since the ability to recognize and promote the best-qualified individuals would show that Lee is a good manager.

Coaching Non-traditional Workers

Purpose: To effectively coach employees whose past experiences, values and expectations differ significantly from those of traditional workers.

Importance: Coaching has always been an important skill for managers. Basically, the effective coach teaches an employee to do a series of tasks of increasing complexity through a two-way communication process. As a result, the employee gradually becomes a more valuable contributor to the company and the team. An elementary principle of teaching any skill is that the teacher must start from the learner's frame of reference. But what if the teacher, or coach, in this case, comes from a different background? What if the coach does not even understand the employee's frame of reference? This chapter will review some basic aspects of coaching any employee, and then provide tips for overcoming differences such as age, race, gender, religion, sexual orientation, physical ability and geographic origin in the coaching relationship. Coaching is especially important for non-traditional employees because these workers may not have had opportunities to learn the corporate culture and to develop the skills required for advancement. If organizations truly intend to capitalize on diversity it will be critical to provide experiences for personal and professional growth.

Step #1 — Sharpen Your Coaching Technique With All Employees.
(Provides a solid foundation for learning to vary your approach in response to different employee characteristics.)
1. Establish a positive relationship with the employee before beginning the process of coaching. Whether you are a successful coach will largely depend on the quality of your prior relationship with that employee. If the employee trusts you, has learned that you will listen, and believes that you genuinely care about his well-being, he is much more likely to follow your instructions, imitate your actions and openly share concerns about the obstacles that prevent him from learning the desired tasks.
2. Follow these steps whenever you coach an employee:
   • Explain the purpose and process of coaching to

the employee.
- Ask the employee what he hopes to achieve in the organization, and explain how the coaching will help him reach his goals. Be sure that he understands that coaching is not a punishment for poor performance, but instead a recognition that he has talents that potentially can benefit the company and the team.
- Express satisfaction for positive past performance (see Chapter 3, Step #1).
- Explain that coaching is a two-way process requiring joint cooperation. In essence, the employee will get out of the process what he is willing to put into it.
- Mutually discuss ideas for the employee's growth, and together develop a plan of action.
- Be sure to listen to the employee's ideas and concerns throughout each meeting (coaches often give excellent direction but forget to listen). Listening is also a good way to support the employee when he is struggling to learn new behavior.
- Offer constructive feedback on an ongoing basis.
- Meet with the employee on a regular basis to evaluate his progress, provide suggestions for improvements and plan for future growth.

Step #2 — Understand The Impact Of Cultural Values On Career Planning And Performance.
(Prepares you to coach non-traditional employees who may have different expectations for relationships, recognition and promotion in the workplace.)

1. Understand your own cultural values. Although we tend to take our own culture for granted, in order to understand how others may differ it is important that you understand your own expectations, and the values that lie at the base of those expectations. In general, different cultures have specific values in four areas that impact career and work life: formality, harmony, conformity, and internal/external control. Following, mainstream (traditional or white North American) cultural values are listed, along with some examples of how these values impact the workplace. Remember that whenever discussing cultural differences, you are discussing groups of people. There will be many individual differences within these groups, since some individuals have been more strongly influenced by their cultural background than others. Beware of turning the cultural information listed below into cultural stereotypes by assuming that it applies to all individuals within those groups!

Every Person Has Been Influenced In Two Ways

Overlap: Extent to which an individual has been influenced by the cultural groups to which he belongs.

Individual Influences (Personality, unique experiences, etc.

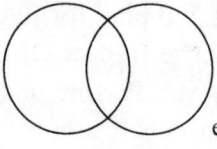

Group Influences (Age, race, gender, heritage, religion, geographic origin, etc.

For people who identify with the norms or values of their cultural heritage there is great overlap between these two circles. For others, there is very little overlap. This can also change over time. For example, Bill grew up in an Irish community. He marries someone of a different heritage and moves out of state. Over the years, Bill will probably "grow away" from his culture.

Knowing about different cultures can help us better understand and communicate with others. If I know that Dawn comes from a Native American tribe that discourages prolonged eye contact, I will not assume she is dishonest just because she does not hold my gaze.

Mainstream North American Cultural Values

Dimension	Mainstream Values	Examples of Impact on Workplace
Formality	Informal, democratic, casual	Employees, managers may be on first-name basis; people casually reveal intimate details about themselves; posture and dress casual
Harmony	"Tell it like it is," conflict acceptable as long as it is not overly emotional	Employees will argue and debate issues even with superiors
Conformity	Individuality rather than conformity	Employees openly compete for positions; self-promotion is expected and rewarded
Internal/ External Control	Internal: self-control, "self-made man"	Career advancement viewed as result of own initiative and talent

hing The Wave Of Workforce Diversity

.. Understand that employees from other cultural groups often differ, as described below. However, take care not to assume that the following information will apply to any individual; just keep it in mind as you communicate to find out whether or not these general cultural observations apply to the person with whom you're working.

Non-Mainstream Values

Dimension	Non-Mainstream Values	Examples of Impact on Workplace
Formality	African-American: Informal (spontaneous) in emotional expression; may share personal information with people of other racial groups only on need-to-know basis.	May be viewed as "too loud" by mainstream employees; may be accused of "stand-offishness" or un-friendliness if unwilling to share personal details with colleagues.
	Hispanic-American: More formal than mainstream culture since pride and honor are important, but values free emotional expression.	May take longer to develop camaraderie in workplace than mainstream but relationships may be deeper once established (managers should take time to develop rapport).
	Asian-American: Very formal, "saving face" (public decorum) extremely important, respect for authority a primary value.	Often think mainstream employees are rude to their superiors, and are appalled at the casual attitude and language used in the typical U.S. company. Managers need to develop rapport very

slowly and use titles (Mr.). Help employee avoid public embarrassment (e.g., ask for questions in writing).

Harmony	African-American: "Tell it like it is," open conflict acceptable	(See comments above under Formality.)
	Hispanic-American: Open and candid but aware of proper place within group.	(No significant difference from mainstream.)
	Asian-American: Harmony and peace essential; open conflict unacceptable.	May do everything possible to maintain group harmony, including not speaking out (which would set oneself apart), and avoiding disagreement at all costs. Public recognition may be humiliating (managers might recognize privately).
Conformity	African-American: Individualistic, values improvisation and self-expression in attire. Ties to family and community strong.	May vacillate between conforming to power structure (as survival mechanism) and "doing own thing" or even conforming to black colleagues as supportive gesture.
	Hispanic-American: Conformity a stronger value than individuality.	More likely to conform or passively "go along" than to assert oneself. Unlikely to promote oneself or talk about own achievements.

	Asian-American: Conformity is a primary value. Role of group more important than individual needs.	Often will not seek promotions, speak up in groups, or share own achievements. Challenge for manager is getting these employees to take initiative.
Internal/ External Control	African-American: More internal than Asian but less than mainstream. Behavior more important than family position in determining worth.	Due to past oppression may have difficulty believing that personal effort will result in advancement. Managers must ensure that consequences are directly linked to performance.
	Hispanic-American: Greater weight on external. Family ties may be more important than personal efforts.	Because of strong family values, managers must be especially sensitive to work-family issues: e.g., ill family members, funerals, child care.
	Asian-American: External orientation strongly influenced by hierarchical political structure and religious beliefs that emphasize destiny.	Employee may have difficulty believing they have personal control over future advancement (since "fate controls").

[Notes: (1) The above listing is not meant to deny the richness of African heritage. The observations regarding African-American values stem largely from the culture of oppression to which Black Americans have been subjected. (2) Comments regarding Hispanic-Americans and Asian-Americans refer primarily to recent immigrants or first-generations citizens. There are countless Americans with Hispanic and Asian surnames who have been in the United States for generations and are very "Americanized." Also, the above discussion is admittedly simplistic, since there are many different Hispanic and Asian "cultures."]

The following scenario illustrates how managers benefit by understanding cultural differences.

Bruce is a manager in a southeastern building supply company. Pedro, who immigrated to the U.S. from Puerto Rico last year, has been with the company for two months. During that time, he has been an excellent employee. He is an especially hard worker, and he seems to be well-liked by all of his co-workers. The only complaint Bruce has about Pedro is his lack of punctuality. Although Pedro knows that his shift begins at 8:00 AM, he is typically 15 to 20 minutes late. Bruce planned to speak with Pedro about his tardiness last Friday, but he put it off because he knows Pedro is very proud and he wanted to take the weekend to consider what he planned to say.

Luckily, he ran into Liz at a party on Saturday night. Liz conducts training sessions for an airline with a hub in Puerto Rico. Bruce happened to mention Pedro's problem to Liz, and Liz began to laugh. "I'll bet I know why Pedro is late. Wait 'til you hear what happened to me when I went to Puerto Rico!" she said. Bruce listened to Liz's story. On Monday morning, Bruce called Pedro into his office. "Pedro, first I want you to know what a good employee you've been. You're our hardest worker, and you really get along great with the other guys, but I've noticed that you've been coming late to work — 15, 20 minutes every morning.

I wonder if there's a problem or some way I can help you."

Pedro looked surprised. "Well ... I did not realize. I mean, in my country...."

Bruce thought back to his conversation with Liz. Liz said when she was in Puerto Rico she had arrived at 7:30 to set up the room for her 8:30 training session. But at 8:30 none of the participants had arrived. Liz wondered if she had the wrong day. 8:45 — and still no one came. Finally, when Liz was about to pack up her things at 8:55, the first participant showed up. Everyone else came by 9:15 and Liz began her presentation at 9:30. When she announced that it was time for their "lunch hour," the participants asked, "Is this a U.S. hour or a Puerto Rican hour?"

Bruce realized that his mind had wandered back to Saturday night. Focusing on Pedro again, he explained that in the U.S., punctuality is very important. He asked Pedro whether he understood. Pedro apologized for being late and assured Bruce that he would be early from now on. Bruce breathed a sigh of relief as Pedro left.

Step #3 — Become Aware Of Personal Biases That Can Affect The Coaching Relationship.

(Helps to prevent misunderstanding caused by personal attitudes that are sometimes outside of conscious awareness.)

1. Ask yourself:
   - If I learned that an employee was a member of the following groups, how would I feel about coaching that employee?
     – Ku Klux Klan
     – NAACP

- Gay and Lesbian Rights Association
- Mexican-American Legal Defense Fund
- National Association for Women
- American Jewish Federation
- Parents Anonymous (a self-help group for parents who have abused a child)
- Alcoholics Anonymous
- Depressives Anonymous
- Any other group memberships that would generate strong feelings?
- How would I feel about coaching an employee who had filed a race, sex or age discrimination lawsuit against his previous employer?
- How would I feel about coaching an employee who is known as a flirt?
- How would I feel about coaching an employee who has a chip on his shoulder because he has experienced discrimination in the past (and now thinks people are mistreating him even when this isn't true)?
- Is there anyone I would not want to coach? What are my reasons? What would I do if it were necessary to coach this person?

2. Do you have any of the following attitudes that might make you hesitate to coach an employee?
   - Coaching takes too much time; a good employee will learn on his own if given a chance. (Although coaching takes time, in the long run it will increase your ability to delegate so you will be able to spend time managing because you will know you can count on your employees to do the

job right.)
- If employees really want my help they should ask for it. (Coaching should be a regular part of your managerial responsibilities. All employees should know that they will be coached at times — sometimes because they request it, and at other times because you recommend it.)
- I don't want employees to depend on me; they need to stand on their own two feet and the best way to learn this is to make a few mistakes. (Employees actually become more self-sufficient after they are coached, especially if the coach builds in opportunities for greater responsibility over a period of time. And rest assured, they will still make a few mistakes.)
- If I spend time coaching one person, the other people in the department will think I am playing favorites. (Providing equal opportunity does not mean you must treat everyone the same. Instead, it means that every employee has an equal chance to develop his skills and abilities through the experiences he needs — coaching, training, mentoring, learn-by-doing and all of the other ways that employees acquire new skills.)
- I am a pretty good technical person, but I'm not much of a teacher. (Take a risk. If you expect the people you supervise to grow by trying new things, it is important that you model this behavior. And don't be afraid to let the employee know you are aware that you are just developing your coaching skills. If you are willing to be

imperfect, it gives employees permission to take a few risks too. Remember, coaching is a key skill for people who really want to be excellent managers.)

Step #4 — Vary Your Coaching Behavior To Accommodate Cultural Differences.

(Increases your effectiveness in coaching diverse employees.)

1. Follow these suggestions to apply the basic coaching steps (covered above in Step #1) to diverse employees:
   - Explain the purpose and process of coaching. Your goal here is to ensure that the employee understands what you will be doing together (e.g., meeting once a week for the next six weeks or so), why this is important (identify the new skills that the employee will be learning), and how the process works (review the eight basic coaching steps.) Refer back to Chapter Six, Step #2 for suggestions about increasing your chances of being understood if the employee speaks limited English, and to Step #3 for tips on assessing whether you've been understood.
   - Ask for their goals and explain how coaching will help them achieve these goals. Here is where your knowledge of cultural differences will come in handy. It is very important not to impose your goals on employees but to listen and ask open-ended questions as they explain what they want to achieve. Hopefully, you will have already established rapport with the employee prior to

beginning the coaching relationship since, as discussed above, people from certain cultures may be less forthcoming with "personal" goals if they do not know and trust you. The goals of some employees may be very simple — just to be a "good employee" — especially if they believe that they have little personal control over the future. Other employee goals may be primarily relationship-oriented, such as the single parent who wants to earn enough to hire a housekeeper so he can spend more time with his children. Others may have very ambitious goals in the company, which you may see as unrealistic. Now is not the time to question those goals: simply help the employee understand how the coaching process will move them a step toward their chosen goals.

- Recognize positive past performance. Although some cultural groups are humiliated by public recognition, since you will be meeting privately there is little likelihood of offending the person by expressing your appreciation for his past efforts. If the employee acts embarrassed or denies that he deserves the praise, quickly move to the next topic by saying something like, "Well, I just wanted you to know I appreciate your good work."
- Explain that coaching requires joint participation. This step can be especially challenging with the timid employee whose culture teaches that workers should basically be seen and not heard. Some workers may see such cooperation as disrespectful of your authority. Try explaining that the

employee's participation will help you do your job more effectively, and make it clear that your success as a manager depends on how much the employee is willing to work with you to achieve the desired goals.
- Discuss ideas and develop a plan of action. Ask lots of open-ended questions if the employee is very quiet or does not volunteer ideas. Pause long enough for him to formulate a response, especially if his command of English is limited. Then paraphrase what he says, adding your own ideas.
- Listen. Go back to Chapter Three, Step #2 for guidelines.
- Offer constructive feedback on an ongoing basis. Remember the importance of helping the Asian-American worker save face: avoid correcting the employee in front of his peers. Also, a person may be unwilling to admit a lack of understanding, because to ask questions might be seen as disrespectful (questions may imply that you have not explained adequately). Likewise, the employee might be unwilling to let you know he has made a mistake, and may actually try to conceal his error as long as possible. For these reasons, asking the employee, "How are you doing?" is often not effective. Instead, ask the worker to show you a sample of the actual work. If there are informal group leaders from the worker's country in the department, request that they assist you by asking questions in meetings, letting newer employees know that this is encouraged. Finally, let the

employee know that he will not be punished for mistakes which are openly admitted, and that mistakes are actually expected when he is learning a new skill.
- Meet to evaluate progress regularly. Keep these meetings focused on your original goals, rather than drifting into discussions of other problems the employee is having. Your primary purpose is to briefly review the employee's accomplishments, recognize special efforts, provide encouragement and suggestions, and set goals for future growth. If you have worked through each of the prior seven steps, this step should proceed smoothly regardless of the employee's gender or culture.

Eight

Motivating and Empowering Diverse Employees

Amanda is the director of nursing at a large suburban hospital. Keith, one of her nursing supervisors, is an African-American man with a true talent both for supervision and nursing. Unlike so many of Amanda's other nurses, he seems to possess the rare combination of technical excellence, a great bedside manner, and attention to details that can make or break a smooth transition from one shift to the next. Amanda is very fond of Keith, and they have had an excellent working relationship.

But lately, Amanda has been hearing through the grapevine that Keith has been frustrated with their last few case conferences. And, to be totally honest with herself, Amanda has not been all that satisfied with Keith's participation at these meetings. It almost seems as if she and Keith have been on a different wavelength lately. Amanda is sure it has nothing to do with their racial difference, since she has experienced smooth relationships with lots of other African-American friends and colleagues. At the same time, *although she only has a handful of male nurses on the staff, she works very well with these men, and in fact, with men in general. Amanda wonders, "What could be going on?" She decides to confront the problem head-on, and asks Keith to meet with her over lunch.*

Amanda begins by sharing how much she appreciates Keith's friendship, and also his nursing abilities. Then she explains her concerns: that she's heard he feels frustrated, and also that she has had a vague sense of discomfort herself following their recent case conferences. She tells Keith that she wants to figure out what is happening, solve the problem and clear the air so they can enjoy working together again. Meanwhile, Keith is looking relieved, and smiling as Amanda continues talking. Finally, Keith replies that he is really glad that Amanda took the initiative to have lunch today, and admits that their past few case conferences have been a source of frustration. Keith says that mainly he feels they need some new procedures, but when he has brought this up at the meetings, Amanda has seemed to ignore him. Amanda stares at Keith. After a moment she laughs and touches her forehead as if the light just went on.

She says, "I've been frustrated because you could not seem to see the big picture — as my friend I expected you to share my vision of where we were going as a hospital. I understand it now, Keith. I'm the big picture person, and you're the person who deals with details. That's how we've complemented each other in the past. The funny thing is that the very thing I appreciate about you is your attention to details — and then I'm frustrated when you do not share my vision! So the bottom line is, I have not been giving you what you really need in order to do your best work. Right?"

Keith smiles. *"I'm sure glad we had this conversation,"* he says.

Empowering Employees

Purpose: To develop effective motivational and empowerment strategies for diverse employees.

Importance: Motivation is directly related to notions of reward and punishment, which reflect personal values — in fact, what is considered rewarding has always been very different for different individuals, even in the traditional workforce. But developing motivators for people of different ages, races, genders and cultural backgrounds can be a real challenge. As we saw in the last chapter, diverse cultures view the world in ways that significantly impact their work attitudes and expectations. The focus of this chapter is not simply motivation: we will go beyond lighting a fire under employees. Rather than just encouraging them to work hard, the goal is empowering them — which builds employee self-esteem and inspires them to work *smart*. This makes it possible for diverse employees to fully use their unique talents and express their unique perspectives, thereby enabling the company to truly capitalize on workforce diversity.

Step #1 — Clearly Communicate That Employee Diversity Can Benefit The Company.
(Lets every employee know that he is appreciated for the special talents, perspectives, skills, and experiences he brings to the organization.)
1. Conduct a team meeting with the purpose of focusing on potential benefits of recognizing, valuing and capitalizing on the diversity within the team. An effective way of accomplishing this is to divide the group into smaller groups of three to five employees each. Then ask them to work together to brain-storm personal, professional and organizational benefits that result from meeting the diverse needs of employees. Have them list these potential benefits on sheets of flipchart paper, giving them 20 to 30 minutes to complete this activity. More specifically, the questions are:
• If we really recognize and value diversity, and meet the needs of every employee, how will we benefit as individuals?
• How will we benefit in our careers — as professionals?
• How will the organization benefit as a whole?

For example, personal benefits include the opportunity to learn about other cultures and parts of the world, to learn other languages, to develop awareness of our own biases and "blind spots," to develop new problem-solving strategies and to become a more well-rounded person. In addition to these (which might also be pluses in our work life), professional benefits include the opportunity to learn leadership and supervisory skills effective with diverse employees, to learn about other countries in preparation for working abroad, to develop interpersonal skills that reduce stress and increase morale and job satisfaction and to become a more effective team player. Organizational benefits include the ability to learn dos, don'ts and taboos from employees in preparation for penetrating diverse markets, eliminating the tremendous cost of grievances and premature terminations, more innovative and collaborative teamwork resulting in increased productivity and managers' ability to focus on high-priority goals rather than on resolving employee conflict.

When the small groups have completed their lists of potential benefits, tape the flipchart pages to a wall and have a spokesperson from each small group present the benefits listed to the large group.

2. The team should now come up with a list of core values about how people will be treated in the work group based on their new awareness that diversity is an advantage. These might include values like respect, trust, open communication, integrity, honesty or quality. Following each value, the team should write a brief descriptive statement beginning with, "We will...." This list of core values thus becomes a code of behavior that members of the team agree to follow. For a sample list of core values consistent with a philosophy of valuing diversity, refer to the Appendix.

3. Practice what you preach. Be sure that, as the manager, your daily behavior exemplifies the values listed in item 2. Remember that you are a powerful model for your people, and that they will be looking to you as an example of how these values can be put into practice.

Step #2 — Follow A Proven Strategy For Empowering All Employees.

(Provides a solid foundation for learning to vary your approach in response to different employee characteristics.)

1. Since empowerment really means "sharing power," consider whether you are truly willing to give up a little short-term control in order to gain a staff that in the long term, will be self-motivated, self-controlled and will demonstrate self-initiative. Although employee empowerment is currently a fad in many organizations, in reality it requires leadership that is willing to risk letting go for a period of time. This does not mean you let employees do whatever they want or adopt a totally relaxed attitude. But it does mean investing extra time and effort in coaching employees and building self-managed teams. It also means recognizing that, initially at least, there is some likelihood that newly empowered employees will make errors, which are rarely fatal and can be transformed into valuable new skills. In essence, empowerment involves building employee self-esteem so that people can use their own personal power to be more creative,

flexible and productive.

The following experience is a great illustration of empowerment in action!

Several years ago my husband and I spent a long Thanksgiving weekend at Tapatio Springs, a golf resort in Texas. Although the service we received throughout our stay was exemplary, a particular incident comes to mind. One morning we went to the restaurant, where a sumptuous breakfast buffet was offered at a special price. Our waitress came over and, as usual, greeted us in an exceptionally pleasant manner. Then she asked if we'd like to try the buffet. I answered that it looked great, but since I like my scrambled eggs well-done, I'd order from the menu. She said, "No problem! If you'd like, we'll cook your eggs in the kitchen, and you can still go to the buffet — at no extra charge, of course!" I was really impressed!

Later I realized that this waitress had been empowered to make this decision. Spontaneously, and without having to check with a supervisor, she responded to my unique needs. She had turned customer diversity into a competitive advantage, especially since I'm still talking about that experience! What great advertising! This kind of personalized service is so unusual that we remember it — and tell our friends about it.

2. Follow these steps to empower all the people on your team:
    - Establish clear goals and directions but be flexible in letting employees use their own methods to accomplish these goals. The key here is to

remember that people process information and solve problems differently. Some members of your team simply need the big picture, a broad outline of what you want to accomplish. Because these people process information from "general to specific," giving them too much detail tends to stifle their creativity. On the other hand, those who think from "specific to general" appreciate being given a step-by-step procedure, including any available data (or sources for getting this data), in order to begin the process of problem-solving. Both of these problem-solving methods have strengths, but they also have weaknesses.

Unfortunately, many managers fail to understand this critical difference in style, and instead assume that everyone else thinks the way they do. The "big picture" manager who fails to give sufficient detail to people who require it will cripple their ability to maximize their most valuable talent — the ability to foresee all the small details and necessary steps to navigate from the beginning of a project to its completion. The "detail" manager who fails to provide "big picture" employees enough leeway for freedom in problem-solving will prevent the "visionary" kind of thinking which is the basis of all innovation and improvement.

How can you know which employees are "detail-oriented" and which are "big picture" people? One way is to ask them whether they prefer being given a broad outline versus a specific procedure to follow before beginning to solve a problem. Of course, the risk here is that many people simply are not aware of how they solve problems. For example, a "detail" person might report that she is "big picture" because although she does not begin with the big picture, eventually she gets there. A more valid way of gaining this insight is to give employees a simple but highly useful test like the *Personal Style Inventory,* developed by William Taggart and Barbara Taggart-Hausladen. Consult the Appendix for ordering information.

Although a major benefit of this test is the knowledge it gives managers of their people, an equally valuable aspect involves the awareness that team members gain of how their own styles may differ from the styles of their co-workers. This enables them to determine whether disagreements are related to differences in gender, culture, or personal style, so that these difficulties are more quickly and easily resolved. It also helps them modify their communication approach to better fit that of their teammates so that they can capitalize on the strengths and compensate for the weaknesses of each other.

- Provide knowledge (skills, training, information) and resources. It's one thing to hire a talented workforce. It's quite another to provide these employees with opportunities to fully develop their talents. In *The New Leaders,* Ann Morrison reports that poor career planning and development

is the second most important barrier in holding back non-traditional managers. She goes on to list eight developmental tools ranked highest by the 16 companies identified as leaders in managing diversity and studied by her team:
1. Diversity training programs
2. Networks or support groups within the organization
3. "Fast track" development programs for high potential employees
4. Informal internal networking activities
5. Job rotation
6. Formal mentoring programs
7. Informal mentoring programs
8. Entry development for newly hired employees designated as high potential.

Although we are discussing non-management employees, efforts like these make it possible for every employee to develop the skills and corporate savvy required for full participation and advancement in the modern workplace. As discussed in the last chapter, you will be personally coaching team members on specific tasks. However, the above development initiatives would likely be carried out without your active involvement (although you might request or organize them in your role as a manager). Also, the programs listed above tend to focus on knowledge and skills that benefit the individual, team and organization over the long term, rather than being required for the employee's current

job.
- Let people know they are valuable to the organization. Sometimes managers assume that people automatically recognize their value. The thinking might be, "If a person still has a job here and gets reasonably positive performance reviews, he must know he's a valuable employee." But would we apply this kind of thinking to customers? We go out of our way to ensure that customers know they're appreciated! We especially want their input — what are we doing well, and what can we do better? Asking employees for feedback is equally important. (Refer to Chapter 5, Step #1 for more information about asking questions that are most likely to elicit this kind of honest feedback.)
- Trust and listen to employees. Why is trust so important? Because trust is a key to communication, and communication is the link that determines whether high job satisfaction will result in high job performance. In their book, *Creating the High-Performance Team,* Steve Buchholz and Thomas Roth summarize the satisfaction-performance research as follows:

Satisfaction	Communication	Performance
high	high	highest
low	high	high
high	low	low
low	low	lowest

The surprising thing about this chart is that, even when employees are dissatisfied with their jobs, if they are able to talk about it their job performance is still high. Also, when employees are highly satisfied but they do not communicate, their job performance is low.

Finally, the authors explain that, "Trust is a prerequisite to high communication. When you do not trust someone, you are unwilling to communicate with them. The major no-trust issue is that people stop communicating. If communication stops, several negative consequences can occur, including confusion, tension, reduction of productivity, resentment, frustration and inability of employees to do the job." Obviously, the best way to engender trust is to be trustworthy. When a manager keeps promises, is honest with employees about the real reasons why a raise is not forthcoming or why certain policies are instituted, and treats employees with genuine respect, it's easy for employees to believe that the manager sincerely cares for their well-being.

- Provide recognition for a job well done. Like parents, managers often ignore employees when they are doing what they are supposed to do, but harshly reprimand employees when they get out of line. We all want to know that our work is appreciated, particularly when we have gone beyond the call of duty or have completed an especially difficult project. Be sure you catch employees doing something right and recognize

their efforts. Although different employees respond to different forms of recognition (as we will discuss later), creative managers use a variety of recognition methods, including verbal praise, written thank-you's, plaques and certificates of achievement, public ceremonies and parties, small work-related gifts (like pens, calendars and paperweights), time off, vacation trips, raises and bonuses, and other monetary rewards. Some organizations actually provide catalogs of gift items that employees can earn through a point system. Whatever method of recognition you choose, be sure to clarify the criteria for earning rewards that go beyond simple verbal or written thank-you's, so you'll avoid the perception of favoritism.
- Give authority, responsibility and accountability. It is amazing how people respond to being given a responsibility that is uniquely theirs. In fact, many employees see this as a form of recognition. Obviously, people must be given the necessary information and resources, as well as the authority to make decisions related to their assigned task. In general, people excel when they are given tasks that they find challenging, but which are still within their abilities. Clearly communicating the importance of the task, information or instructions needed to complete it, and specifications or standards of quality are also critical to ensure that the employee expects, and then experiences, a successful outcome.
- Encourage teamwork. Make it clear that you

expect people to work together on tasks, especially those that require problem-solving or creative thinking. Communicate to team members that the goal is for them to capitalize on the strengths and compensate for the weaknesses of each other. Then, remember to recognize people for working together, since actions which are acknowledged will tend to be repeated.
- Respect individual and cultural differences. As discussed in Chapter Seven, the uniqueness in each person results from an interaction of psychology (individual factors such as heredity, personality, education and intelligence, personal experiences, physical ability/disability) and sociology (group factors such as race, gender, age/generation, geographic origin, creed, socioeconomic status, family background). Most of us are pretty good at recognizing psychological differences, thanks to all the self-help books and articles published in the past few decades. But we tend to underestimate the importance of sociology, all of the different factors that define our culture — those common beliefs and customs we have learned from society about what is and what should be. One reason we do not appreciate the impact of culture is that most cultural learning occurs outside of conscious awareness. We absorb cultural knowledge much as a sponge absorbs water. As a result, it never occurs to us that someone may be acting strangely because of a cultural difference. (Despite my expertise in this

area, whenever I communicate with my mother-in-law, whose heritage is Polish-American, I'm challenged by my own tendency to forget the importance of cultural differences.)

In Step #3, we will look at some motivational tips for managing culturally diverse employees. Obviously, though, there is no way to address every cultural variation. In Chapter Seven we considered some general communication differences for several major U.S. racial groups. To address motivation of specific cultural groups would be misleading for two reasons. First, motivation is almost as individual as a thumbprint. The more you, the manager, are able to connect with each individual employee, the more you will understand what it will take to ignite his passion to excel. Also, the complexity of workforce diversity grows at an accelerating pace. In a recent training session composed of 18 people, one woman had immigrated from Samoa, one man was from French Guiana, and another man had cerebral palsy (and attended the workshop with his canine companion). No amount of pre-reading would have prepared me for the diversity in that class.

Step #3 — More Tips For Empowering Culturally Diverse Workers.
(Applies specialized skills to the above eight-step process.)
1. Clearly communicate your expectations, verbally

and in writing. Although managers often assume that employees know what is expected, remember that expectations are usually culturally-determined. As a result, foreign-born workers often are not aware that they should take initiative, express complaints, admit their lack of understanding, seek promotions, talk about their achievements or even speak English in the workplace. Of course it is important not to appear condescending or to treat workers like children, so the best course of action may be to say to the team, "Many of these points are probably obvious to you, but let's cover them anyway just in case your last manager had different expectations."

Then go over your list of expectations, giving the rationale and at least one specific example for each item. Also, ask the open-ended, "What questions do you have before we move on?" This should follow your discussion of each expectation. It's also a good idea to ask team members what else they think needs to be added for the team to work together effectively. People are usually more receptive to expectations when the manager has requested their input, rather than forcing the rules down their throats.

2. Use culturally-appropriate methods of positive reinforcement. Since workers from other cultures may be uncomfortable with public recognition, discuss your plans for recognizing them before planning a public ceremony. Simply let them know you really appreciate their special efforts, and you would like

to give them some recognition. Then tell them you are considering organizing a special event to recognize employees. Let them know that you are aware that in some cultures, people are embarrassed by this kind of public recognition, and ask them if they would prefer to be recognized in private, or if they are comfortable with being recognized in a group ceremony. If they indicate that they would prefer private recognition, consider written recognition (for example, a framed certificate or plaque), which you could present privately, and which they could display in the privacy of their own office or home. If the entire team was involved in accomplishing a certain result, recognize everyone on the team simultaneously. The point is to avoid singling out the worker who would experience a loss of face.

Several years ago we interviewed the employees at a large high-tech manufacturing facility. The question to be answered was: Is diversity training needed to assist the employees in developing better working relationships and solving intercultural conflicts, considering the organization's predominantly Asian workforce? During the interviews we discovered that the company had initiated small creative problem-solving groups. The reward for generating the greatest number of creative ideas was the opportunity to present these ideas to management and receive public recognition for these efforts. Unfortunately, the designer of this program had not realized that this reward would probably not be motivational for the Asian workers.

On the contrary, during the interviews we learned that the Asian employees hated having to present their ideas, and they would do almost anything to avoid the embarrassment of this kind of recognition. Although public recognition is often a significant motivator for traditional employees, more than diversity training, this company needed to consider the values of its non-traditional workforce. Instead, its good intentions to motivate its people were having the opposite effect.

3. Encourage employees to want to change. Respecting employees' cultural heritage does not mean that you have to let them do whatever they choose. For example, if a person comes from a culture in which time is treated very casually, and he repeatedly comes to work late, it is important to let him know that, in this country (and in this company), punctuality is crucial for the person who wants to succeed. You will begin by meeting with him and expressing appreciation for some positive behavior (assuming that you can do this honestly). Then, you will share your observation that he has been coming in late. (Remember the anecdote about the Puerto Rican employee?) Next, you will wait for an explanation (since the tardiness may be a result of something other than his cultural beliefs). Finally, if the person's explanation seems to suggest that he simply does not know how important it is to be punctual, use this opportunity to educate him about the consequences of tardiness in the U.S. Also, emphasize that you see his cultural heritage as an

asset — it gives him a different perspective in solving problems, and that is a real plus. So you have no desire to change his entire cultural experience but only this one particular behavior.

4. Accurately understand the behavior. Use your questioning and listening skills (see Chapter 3) to determine what an employee actually did and the motives behind it. If change is necessary, decide whether you are dealing with an individual difference or a cultural difference so you will be able to plan the most effective motivational strategy. (Refer to Chapter Seven, Step #2 for a discussion of these two kinds of differences.) Check your local library for more specific information about particular cultural groups, including their values and communication patterns. Also, Chapter Seven suggests methods of coaching culturally diverse employees.

5. Compromise when possible. Learn to speak the employee's cultural language. If you know that group harmony or saving face is an important value, use these terms in explaining the benefits of expected employee behavior. Remember that people always want to know, "What's in it for me?" The more workers perceive that their goals are consistent with your goals for the team as a whole, the more motivated they will be to fully cooperate. If an employee makes an unusual request that is related to his cultural heritage, be as flexible as possible in granting that request. For example, some employees request time off for religious holidays which are not commonly observed in the United States. Perhaps

that employee would be willing to work, instead, on Christmas or some other holiday which we observe in this country. Remember:

Treating people equally does not mean treating everyone the same. It means everyone has an equal chance to have his needs met, even though those needs may differ.

6. Find out what people need. Have each individual on your team rank the following needs on a scale of one to ten:
   - Job security
   - Being given more responsibility over a period of time
   - Financial security
   - Professional growth
   - Power/ability to influence decision-making
   - Opportunity to contribute to the company or to society
   - Recognition and respect
   - Autonomy/freedom to be creative
   - Structure/knowing specific guidelines in advance
   - Flexibility of hours to spend time with family

Be sure to let employees know that there are no right or wrong answers to this exercise. You simply want to understand them better so that you can better meet their needs.

Nine

Improving Communication Between Men and Women

Harry is a vice president at a Midwestern bank. He has been looking for a new human resource specialist, and today he has scheduled to interview Betty. When Betty arrives, Harry thanks her for coming in and launches into a description of the job requirements for the position. Betty asks thoughtful questions and seems to appreciate Harry's feelings of urgency in finding someone for this new position. He asks her about her former experience, and Betty outlines more than 15 years of banking experience. Harry is beginning to think Betty is definitely the person for this job.

Then Harry explains that the bank has recently implemented an innovative community outreach program, and asks Betty if she has ever been involved in anything similar. Betty enthusiastically replies that she herself spearheaded this kind of program at her previous bank. Then she describes who the program was aimed at, how it was implemented, how the bank's staff were involved, how it benefitted the community, and on and on. Harry wonders why Betty won't just get to the point, and he begins to think that maybe she may not be the person for the job after all. At the end of the interview, Harry says he will be in touch with Betty.

The following day he hires a solid, but uninspiring, man who worked in human resources in another state. A month later, Harry attends a reception where he meets a friend from a neighboring bank. His friend excitedly explains that he recently hired a human resource person named Betty — and she is the best employee he's ever had! In the short time she has been with the bank, she has proposed and implemented a new program that is projected to bring in over a million dollars in the next year!

Poor Harry. If only he had known that Betty's tendency to provide elaborate details was simply part of a very common gender-based communication pattern, he could have been the one boasting about his new employee.

Capitalizing On Gender Differences

Purpose: To improve working relationships between men and women and resolve conflict that is primarily due to gender differences.

Importance: Although most of us would agree that men and women communicate differently, the question is, "How can we bridge this communication gap?" This chapter will make you aware of the different communication styles typically used by many men and women, and suggests several ways to enhance workplace communication between the genders. This information is especially important with the influx of men and women into jobs that had traditionally been reserved for the other gender, and with the increased likelihood that teams in all functional areas will include people of both genders. In addition, since gender stereotypes are often the root of sexual harassment, it is essential that modern managers increase their gender awareness in order to create a workplace where employees feel respected as people and as professionals.

Step #1 — Teach Your Employees That Men And Women Come From Different Cultures, With Different Languages
(Provides awareness that is prerequisite to learning adaptive behavior.)
1. Research shows that, growing up in the U.S., men and women have very different social experiences. Since they have learned different survival messages, different values, different beliefs, different expectations and different communication patterns, relationships between men and women are conducted as cross-cultural communication. The way to be more effective in any cross-cultural situation is to begin to truly understand the other person. This happens in two ways: by learning about his culture, and by learning about individual characteristics and experiences. Once this understanding occurs, we are able to begin to complement each other (that is, to capitalize on the differences).

2. The primary survival messages received by men and women, which affect their communication styles are:

Men	Women
Survival Messages:	*Survival Messages:*
Compete, Win, Solve the Problem	Relate, Understand, Nurture

Examples of Impact on Communication:	*Examples of Impact on Communication:*

When Someone Else Has A Problem:

He focuses on facts, offers help and gives advice	She focuses on feelings, listens and probes for more information

When Making Decisions:

He rarely asks for help and often makes unilateral decisions	She more often asks for help and makes collaborative decisions

When Discussing Issues:

He under-explains	She over-explains

When Presenting Information:

He lectures (may not involve others) and is more authoritative and concise	She facilitates the involvement of others and is less assertive (uses more qualifiers and disclaimers)

When Discussing Personal Relationships:

He prefers to be vague, considers it disloyal to discuss intimacies	She is more likely to share intimate details of relationships

When Talking With Friends:

He uses more general humor and tends to discuss sports, business and money	She's more likely to use self-effacing humor, and tends to discuss people, feelings and relationships

NOTE: These are generalizations about men and women as two distinct cultural groups. Remember that in any group there will be many individual differences. Also, neither of these styles is right or wrong. They each have strengths and weaknesses in the workplace, and are most effective when used together.

Step #2 — Encourage Your Team Members To Adapt To The Communication Needs of The Other Gender (Begin to bridge the gender gap.)

1. In a team meeting, divide the men and women into two groups and have them work together to list the most persistent communication problems between the genders. Then list your results on a flipchart. How do they compare with the following study by Judith Tingley? She found that 500 men and women said that:
   - Men are more authoritarian than women
   - Women are more emotional than men
   - Men don't take women seriously

   Clearly, both genders can learn new skills to be more effective communicators. This will also make them better able to work together to benefit from their communication differences. Ask your team what new skill areas are indicated by their answers. Tingley's research suggests that:
   - Men need to work on becoming more effective listeners (practicing eye contact and other non-verbal indicators of attention, postponing advice-giving, paraphrasing, reflecting feelings, asking open questions, summarizing).

- Women need to work on becoming more assertive (stating their opinions more concisely and forcefully, eliminating self-effacing humor and similar behaviors like disclaimers, qualifiers and apologizing for their ideas).

The following scenario illustrates the dilemma faced by men and women who differ from traditional gender roles.

One of my clients is a public-sector organization with a large number of women in jobs traditionally held by men. Many of these women have learned that, to survive, they must adapt. Unfortunately, though, sometimes there are also negative consequences when someone essentially takes on the role of the other gender. The case of Paula illustrates the kind of challenge faced by these women. (As with the other cases in this book, Paula's identity and actual profession are disguised.)

Paula is a mail carrier. She especially likes being outdoors and meeting the people on her route. Her only complaint is the attitude of some of her co-workers. In the past, they would either make statements like, "Why aren't you home in the kitchen?" or completely exclude Paula from their conversations. Paula realized that if she was going to be satisfied in her job, she would have to find a way to communicate with these men.

So she started joking around with them — at times using crude language. She was careful not to talk about women's interests or feelings. She even took an evening class in assertiveness. Paula's efforts paid off. She has better relationships with her male co-workers, and there are also more female carriers now. But the same men who criticized or avoided her in the past now call her "Paul, the little man." Although Paula sometimes feels she is in a no-win situation, she has decided that, for now at least, she will ignore their jibes. Since she likes her job, she feels that the rewards outweigh an occasional irritating remark. She also recognizes that as her co-workers get to know and respect her they will be more likely to treat her as an individual.

2. Encourage team members to be more open in asking for what they need. For example,
   - Men can ask women to be concise when time is critical. Before beginning a discussion, the man can say, "By the way, I'm really working on a tight deadline, so this'll have to be quick!"
   - Women can ask men to just listen instead of giving advice. When the woman needs to ventilate, she can say, "I'd really appreciate it if you'd just be a great listener and let me get this off my chest!"
3. To bridge any communication gap, people must share more information, ask more questions and listen more. In their book, *Men and Women: Partners at Work,* Simons and Weissman describe a strategy for increasing openness called "Ask and Tell." This strategy is an excellent way of improving communication with anyone — whether you are communicating with someone of a different age, race, gender or someone from a different region of the world. Briefly, the authors recommend that men and women should ask and tell each other about:

Thoughts and Feeling.
>   Ask: What does this mean to you?
>   How do you feel about this?
>   Tell: I have a sense that ....
>   Here's how I imagine that: ....

Situations.
>   Ask: What do you think might happen?
>   What's going on?
>   Tell: What I foresee is that ....
>   When that happens I usually ....

Potential Opportunities
>   Ask: What opportunities do you see in ...?
>   What do you see yourself doing about ...?
>   Tell: I have a dream that ....
>   There's a chance that ....

Barriers
>   Ask: What's standing in the way?
>   What's missing in order to ...?
>   Tell: I think we need to ....
>   Here's what I'm faced with: ....

Commitments
>   Ask: What's your investment in this?
>   What agreements have you made?
>   Tell: I'm committed to ....
>   I'm responsible for ....

Options
   Ask: What do you see as the pros and cons?
          What else could we do?
   Tell: On the other hand, maybe we could ....
          Let's speculate for a moment ....

Step #3 — Communicate The Legal Definition, Consequences And Company Policy For Sexual Harassment.
(Presents steps toward preventing sexual harassment.)
1. Post the following definitions in a location where everyone will see them several times a day:
   • Sexual Harassment –
   Unwelcome Behavior Of A Sexual Nature
   Two Types of Sexual Harassment
   • Quid Pro Quo Harassment
     Harassment in which employment decisions or special privileges are offered in exchange for sexual favors
   • Environmental Harassment
     Harassment in which unwelcome sexual conduct creates an intimidating, hostile or offensive work environment
2. Ask your human resources professional to schedule a sexual harassment training session. There are excellent video resources available on the topic. At the very least this training should cover the range of behaviors included under quid pro quo and environmental harassment, the difference between flirtation and sexual harassment and what options an

employee has if she thinks she is being harassed. (Note that men can also be the victims of sexual harassment.) Also, employees should have an opportunity to discuss reasons why sexual harassment might go unreported, types of situations in your workplace that might constitute sexual harassment and what employees can do if they suspect that a co-worker is being sexually harassed.

3. Since stereotypes contribute to a harassing environment (for example; "all men have a one-track mind" and "all women who wear provocative clothing are looking for sex"), make it clear to employees that people will be treated as unique individuals, not as stereotypes. Also be sure that employees know that no type of harassment will be tolerated in your workplace, including harassment based on age, race, gender, physical disability, geographic origin, sexual orientation, religion or cultural heritage. Refer back to Chapter Four for working with your team to develop ground rules for appropriate communication.

Ten

Defusing, Managing and Mediating Intercultural Conflicts

Roger is marketing manager for the small tools division of a woodworking products company. The company has developed a new tool that will be exported to the Philippines next year. May and Tony have been assigned to head up this project. Tony is a Filipino employee who immigrated to the U.S. a year ago. Not only does he have a knack for marketing, but his knowledge of the Filipino culture will be invaluable on this project. May recently transferred to the department. She has developed a reputation for being the best at coordinating overseas projects, although she knows little about the Philippines. Unfortunately, May and Tony are currently having a feud, which is seriously interfering with their ability to work cooperatively. May was supposed to develop a document and then get Tony to translate it. But when May and Tony met, Tony was deeply offended because May used a "bossy" tone of voice, and he believes it is not respectful for women to speak to men in that fashion.

As the supervisor of the two feuding people, Roger began his intervention by encouraging May and Tony to work out the problem on their own. But two weeks passed and no real progress was made. Roger then met with May and Tony separately to get more information. From May's perspective, she was simply doing her job. She expressed the conviction that if Tony is going to work in the United States, he should get used to the way things are done here, and that he needs to have more respect for his female colleagues. Tony is insulted and feels that May owes him an apology. He has gone so far as to suggest that, if May must be involved in the project, Roger should assign someone else to take his place. Roger replied that he believes Tony is a key to the project's success. Roger knows that simply directing May and Tony to start working together again — "or else" — is not the answer, since it will not give them a chance to deal with their feelings or develop the skills to resolve similar problems in the future.

This morning on his way to work, Roger heard a radio program about mediation as a problem-solving approach. The program emphasized that a mediator's goal is to help the parties find common ground, and he realizes that May and Tony do have something in common — they both want to be respected. He wonders whether mediation is the best way to restore their relationship. Roger decides to contact the mediator who was interviewed on the radio; after a brief phone conference the mediator agrees to assist Roger in mediating the dispute between May and Tony. Roger later learns that, not only is mediation successful in resolving this conflict, it is a skill that will give him a significant edge in facing future management challenges.

Transform Obstacles Into Opportunities

Purpose: To prevent disagreement from becoming destructive, to turn conflicts into an opportunity for creative problem-solving and to assist employees in resolving differences in a way that enhances working relationships.

Importance: Do the people in your workplace respect each other? Are they genuinely interested in learning more about each other? Do people really listen and express themselves in a way that increases understanding? If so, your need for excellent conflict management skills will be greatly minimized. However, disagreement is not all bad, and in fact can be expected if people are really being open about their ideas and concerns. The goal of this final chapter, then, is to provide you with skills to turn obstacles (that is, disagreement and conflict) into opportunities for greater learning and creativity in the work group.

Step #1 — Help Your Team Members Recognize The Strengths And Weaknesses Of Their Personal Conflict Management Styles.
(Describes five different ways to handle conflict and when each is most appropriate.)
1. Research *(Thomas-Kilmann Conflict Styles)* shows that people typically respond to conflict situations by using one of the following styles:

- Competing: Using whatever it takes to win the other person to my own way of thinking. Expressed by the sentiment, "Winning isn't the most important thing — it's the only thing!" If I use this style, I will usually satisfy my own needs even if this means doing so at the expense of yours.
  - Strengths: Useful in emergencies when quick, decisive action is needed or when company policy prescribes a course of action, so there is no room for compromise.
  - Weaknesses: Discourages openness and damages relationships if used frequently.
- Avoiding: Not addressing the issue at all. Expressed by the sentiment, "It's better to let sleeping dogs lie." If I use this style, I will not satisfy my own needs or your needs.
  - Strengths: Useful when an issue is too trivial to justify argument, when I am extremely emotional and need to regain my composure, when I need to get more information before the discussion or when the potential damage of confrontation outweighs its benefits.
  - Weaknesses: Issues go unresolved and people sweep negative feelings under the carpet, which damages morale and problem-solving.
- Collaborating: Taking the time and effort to find a solution that fully satisfies both of us. Expressed by the sentiment, "One hand washes the other." If I use this style, I am concerned about finding a "win-win" outcome, where your needs are met as

well as mine. (The conflict resolution approach discussed in Chapter Four, Step #3 is based on the collaborating style.)
– Strengths: Useful when both sets of concerns are too important to be compromised, when different perspectives on a problem can contribute to innovative solutions, when consensus is important to increase commitment or when people have strong feelings that have been interfering with the relationship.
– Weaknesses: Requires a high level of trust and usually takes more time than the other approaches, and so should be used only on significant issues that warrant the effort.
- Accommodating: Letting you have your way. Expressed by the sentiment, "You've got to go along to get along." If I use this style, I am concerned about satisfying your needs, even at the expense of my own.
– Strengths: Useful when your concerns are more critical than mine, when preserving harmony and avoiding disruption are especially important or when junior people need to be allowed to learn from mistakes.
– Weaknesses: Frequent use of this approach can undermine self-esteem, decrease problem-solving by too much deference, contribute to undisciplined workers (when used by a manager) and create frustration because my own needs are not being met.
- Compromising: Finding a middle ground

position. Expressed by the sentiment, "I'll scratch your back if you'll scratch mine." If I use this style, I am willing to give up something if I can get something else, so your needs and mine are partially satisfied.

– Strengths: Useful when goals are moderately important and competition may be disruptive, but are not worth the time to collaborate. Also useful when two opponents have mutually exclusive goals and equal power, or when temporary settlements are needed on complex issues.

– Weaknesses: Since neither my needs nor yours are fully satisfied, we will both feel somewhat frustrated, and when used frequently, can create cynicism and damage morale. Also focuses on short-lived solutions rather than long-term, big-picture objectives.

How would this information be valuable to your team? Despite the fact that these five styles are all useful in certain situations, most people have a preferred style that they use almost exclusively. As we will discuss below, in some cases their choice of style is related more to personality, and in other cases, cultural background is the deciding factor. The important point, though, is that the ability to effectively manage conflict is hampered by having access to only one or two styles.

2. A first step, then, is to distribute the above information to your team members. Request that they read it and rank, on a scale of one to five, which style they use most often (#1) down to the style they use least

often (#5).

Call a team meeting to review the styles and ask team members to discuss which styles they use most often, which styles are most difficult for them to use and why. This kind of open discussion is beneficial since it encourages team members to help each other problem-solve more effectively. For example, if someone usually uses a "competing" style but recognizes that she needs to work on learning to compromise, another team member can remind hereof this when they get into an actual conflict situation where compromising is the most appropriate style.

Managers should also help team members recognize that certain conflict management styles may be especially difficult for diverse employees, because these approaches would essentially violate the basic values or norms of their cultural heritage. These intercultural aspects of conflict management are discussed in Step #2.

Step #2 — Teach Team Members Intercultural Problem Solving.

(Suggests tips for overcoming cultural barriers in conflict management.)

1. In Asian, Middle Eastern and Filipino cultures a primary value is to preserve the social balance. Since people coming from these backgrounds place a high premium on harmony, employees from these cultures may tend to avoid negative confrontation. They may attempt to save face for all parties by relying on either the avoidance or accommodation

styles. As a manager, you can help these workers appreciate the importance of more assertive modes like compromising and collaborating. For example, you might point out that avoidance and accommodation may preserve harmony for a short time, but when feelings and concerns are not expressed they can later erupt and cause greater dissension in the work group.
2. When people have experienced past discrimination, they may see conflict as evidence of prejudice. One way to avoid this perception is to emphasize that conflict is a positive indicator that people are being honest, and that it is often the basis for creativity, innovation and growth. Maintaining an open door is also essential, since people are unlikely to express their suspicions of prejudice to the offending co-worker but may be willing to bring that concern to you. In this case, listening is an important first step. An especially effective approach in this situation is mediation, which will be discussed at the conclusion of this chapter.
3. Often, intolerance of differences can be the cause of conflict. In general, people who feel good about themselves are less likely to be intolerant of the differences in others. The best way to change intolerant attitudes is to provide positive contacts with diverse co-workers over a period of time. But what happens when there is turnover in the work group? The first step is to provide new employees with copies of the team's ground rules (see Chapter Four, Step #1) and core values (see Chapter Eight, Step

#1.) On a continuous basis, encourage employees to complete projects based on their unique talents. Make frequent comments about the value of differences during team meetings. Finally, if it becomes clear that an employee's intolerant attitudes are causing divisiveness, take immediate action: begin by expressing your concerns in a private meeting with the employee. Listen to his side of the story, and determine whether the person is motivated to change. If so, provide a strong warning and require the employee to counsel with a diversity consultant and/or attend diversity awareness and a communication skills training program (your human resources professional should be able to provide a list of available classes).

Step #3 — Act As A Mediator To Resolve Intercultural Conflicts

(Describes a strategy for resolving co-worker conflicts, improving long-term working relationships and enhancing employees' intercultural competence.)

1. Christopher Moore, author of *The Mediation Process,* describes mediation as follows:

    Mediation involves the intervention of an acceptable, impartial and neutral third party who has no authoritative decision-making power to assist contending parties in voluntarily reaching their own mutually acceptable settlement of issues in dispute. As with negotiation, mediation leaves the decision-making power in the hands of the people in conflict. Mediation is a voluntary process in that the participants must be willing to accept the assistance of the intervenor if the dispute is to be resolved. Mediation is usually initiated when the parties no longer believe that they can handle the conflict on their own.

When employees are unable to resolve a conflict on their own by using the strategy described in Chapter Four, Step #3, you may choose to act as a mediator. However, as a manager, you are obviously not without that decision-making power referred to by Christopher Moore. Although this creates a special challenge, mediation can still be a very effective tool, assuming that you have already established a moderate degree of trust with your employees. So your first challenge will be to convince them that you are playing the role of a neutral third party in this particular situation, and that your intention is not to tell them what to do, but rather to simply assist in problem-solving. You will also state your belief that, with the help of mediation, they will be able to come to a resolution that satisfies both of them.

2. Once you have clarified your role — that is, explained that you are acting as a neutral mediator (not a decision-maker), follow these steps:
- Explain the limits of confidentiality. This means that you agree not to share the content of the discussion with the employee's co-workers, and you request that the parties also agree to keep the conversation confidential. You also agree not to reveal the discussion to other managers unless the

information requires you to take some action that involves other management-level employees. (For example, you might learn during the discussion that another employee's behavior violated company policy, and it would be your responsibility to inform his or her manager of this fact.)
- Explain the process of mediation and the meaning of "caucus." In this step, you will simply explain what's about to happen: that you will ask one person to share his viewpoint while the other person sits quietly and listens without interrupting. Then, when that person is finished, and you are sure you have a clear picture of that person's perspective, the other person will have a chance to tell his side of the story, while the first speaker listens quietly. Then, after you are sure you understand both points of view, you will try to help both parties come to some agreement or compromise. You also may decide to "caucus" with one or both of them: this means that if the discussion gets too hot or if you need to get other information of a personal nature, you may ask them to meet with you privately for a short time. If this happens, whatever they tell you in private will be confidential — you will not share it with the other person.
- Have one person explain his viewpoint, and ask the other person if he is willing to listen without interrupting. If one person appears to be the injured party, it is common to begin with that person. (If at any time the listener interrupts,

gently tell him to hold on, since he will have a chance to speak in a moment.)
- Ask questions for clarification of issues, feelings, cultural differences and goals (what does he want to happen?) Paraphrase as needed.
- Thank the speaker for his openness and the listener for his cooperation in being silent.
- Have the other person explain his viewpoint while the first speaker listens silently.
- Ask questions and paraphrase as needed; thank both parties again.
- If it is clear that cultural differences are contributing to the dispute, describe the problem as understood in both cultures.
- Find a common ground: for example, "So it sounds like you both really want to work this out because ... and the thing that's standing in the way is ...."
- Ask the first speaker what he is willing to do to resolve the problem; paraphrase; repeat with second speaker; paraphrase again.
- Suggest areas of agreement or compromise.
- Ask for agreement; have parties sign written agreement.

NOTE: If at any time the discussion becomes too emotionally charged or you believe there are pertinent issues which either person is unwilling to discuss openly, ask both parties to caucus individually with you. Then bring them together again.

Several years ago I had the opportunity to assist in mediating a community dispute. The local housing authority had built low-income units in an upper-middle-income neighborhood and teens who lived in the housing units had been accused of loitering, stealing from local convenience stores and generally creating a disturbance. The parents of these teens complained that their children had been harassed by the police and targeted as the likely suspects whenever a crime was committed in the neighborhood.

Assembled around the mediation table were the police, school principals, small business owners, concerned citizens on both sides of the conflict, the housing residents and representatives of the housing authority. We met bi-weekly for 12 weeks. Despite the hostility expressed by both sides in the initial stages of the mediation, it was exciting to observe the parties begin to truly understand each other and finally come to an amicable resolution at the end of 12 weeks.

Not only were the issues resolved, but the individuals developed mutual respect, and in some cases actually became friends. I believe that mediation is the only process that could have had such a positive outcome, considering the strong feelings on both sides of the issue and the vast individual and cultural differences among the parties. There is no magic pill for resolving intercultural disputes, but the synergy generated in a skillfully-handled mediation can potentially heal old wounds while creating new bonds.

Eleven

From Different to Exceptional: Creating A Climate for Growing

From 1982 until 1991, I operated a private practice as a psychologist. I evaluated children and adults to determine the roots of their problems, counseled with children, families, adults, and couples, and acted as an expert witness in forensic cases. By 1986 I had already begun to provide consulting services to organizations on a part-time basis. The opportunity to work in both of these environments resulted in a powerful new insight: all human systems, regardless of size, operate according to the same basic principles. The patterns of dysfunction that I had seen so often in families were played out, on a larger scale, in dysfunctional companies.

In addition, not only did human problems present themselves in similar ways, but the solutions to those problems also were similar. I was more than a little excited to realize that I could use the skills I had developed in a private practice setting to create more functional "families" in the workplace. Having always been more fascinated by human possibilities than by human problems, I asked myself, "What kind of environment, or climate, brings out the best in people? When the counseling relationship works to unleash a person's potential, what's really going on?" I knew that once I described that "climate for growing," I could use my skills to help organizations duplicate it in the workplace. To understand how I finally answered these essential questions, let us look at an especially challenging case from my early years in private practice.

One of my first clients was Brandon, an eight-year-old boy brought to my office by his parents, who complained that he was an "impossible child." They were totally frustrated, explaining that he refused to follow rules at home and at school would kick and bite his little sister every time he got the chance, and refused to go to bed at night, screaming on the floor when told it was bedtime. They already had read several books on handling misbehavior, and had tried, to no avail, to deal with Brandon's behavior by using a system of rewards and punishments. Although they seemed to be "doing everything right," Brandon's behavior only seemed to worsen. My evaluation showed that Brandon had extremely low self-esteem. At school he had been picked on by the other children because he wore a hearing aid. The angrier he became, the more his behavior deteriorated. And as he began to get negative feedback from his teachers and parents about his actions, he responded by "proving" that they were right: he was an impossible child!

I began to see Brandon on a weekly basis. After the first play therapy session with Brandon, I wondered if I could really help him. But his parents reported that he could not wait for his next session with "Dr. Joy," so I decided to hang in there and continue working with him. Since he refused to discuss his problems, we spent our sessions playing games: checkers, ball darts, tic tac toe and nerf basketball. After a couple of weeks I was able to get Brandon to agree to spend the first 15 minutes of our hour discussing his problems at home and at school, as long as I agreed to play games for the remainder of the session. After six weeks, when there had still been no obvious improvement, I began to wonder if Brandon's parents were wasting their time and money. As a new psychologist, I secretly feared that I did not know what I was doing, and thought Brandon should probably be seeing someone more experienced. But Brandon's parents seemed confident that I could help him, since he "loved me so much."

So we continued our sessions. Sometimes we played board games, and Brandon would usually cheat. I pointed out to him that this was not much fun for me since I could never win, but this did not seem to matter to Brandon. After I had been seeing Brandon for about 12 weeks, I scheduled another session with his parents, planning to give them a referral to another psychologist. Although I dreaded this conference, I felt it was unprofessional to continue working with Brandon, since he did not seem to be making any progress. The evening of our conference, I considered getting sick but finally summoned my courage and invited his parents into my office. I began by hesitantly asking them if there were any new developments, thinking that they would surely report Brandon's latest escapades, and fully expecting them to fire me. I was amazed when they beamed: Brandon's mother said she had received a call from his teacher the day before, saying that Brandon had been wonderful in school for the past three weeks. The teacher was astounded at the change in Brandon, and encouraged the parents to keep doing whatever they were doing, because it was working The parents also told me Brandon had not attacked his sister for a long time, and although bedtime was still a minor problem, he was following the rules at home with only occasional outbursts. I tried to conceal my surprise, acting as if I knew all along that Brandon would improve. The parents thanked me profusely for "working a miracle" with their son. After that, I began to see Brandon every other week, then every month, and finally, six months after our first session, Brandon and I tearfully said goodbye to each other. He even brought me a card he had made telling me how much he loved me and would miss seeing me.

What had happened to turn this "impossible child" into a sweet, loving little boy? Although it took a long time to really understand the answer, looking back I believe I simply provided a special kind of environment, a "climate" in which Brandon was free to change and grow, free to be not just different, but exceptional. In the years that followed, I had many similar experiences in private practice. And occasionally, I have had the opportunity to observe the kind of workplace climate that truly brings out the best in every employee (regardless of age, race, gender, physical disability, geographic origin, sexual orientation, creed or any other form of classification).

One of the lessons I learned from these early years is that what we do or say is often less important than how we do what we do or say what we say. Another way to think about this is that perspectives can be more useful than prescriptions. This may be a strange thing to say in the final chapter of a book about skills. But all the skills in the world are useless if we do not really care about our fellow human beings. The question then becomes, "If I truly want to meet the needs of my employees, what kind of environment should I strive to create?"

First, we need to determine whether we are working (or living) in a functional, as opposed to dysfunctional, human system. Put very simply, a functional environment enables us to meet our needs. Only when our more basic needs are met are we able to grow from a lower to a higher level of development. Abraham Maslow believed that every person has five internal needs that provide the motivation to grow. When a lower-level need is satisfied, we are internally motivated to move up to a higher-level need. These needs are:

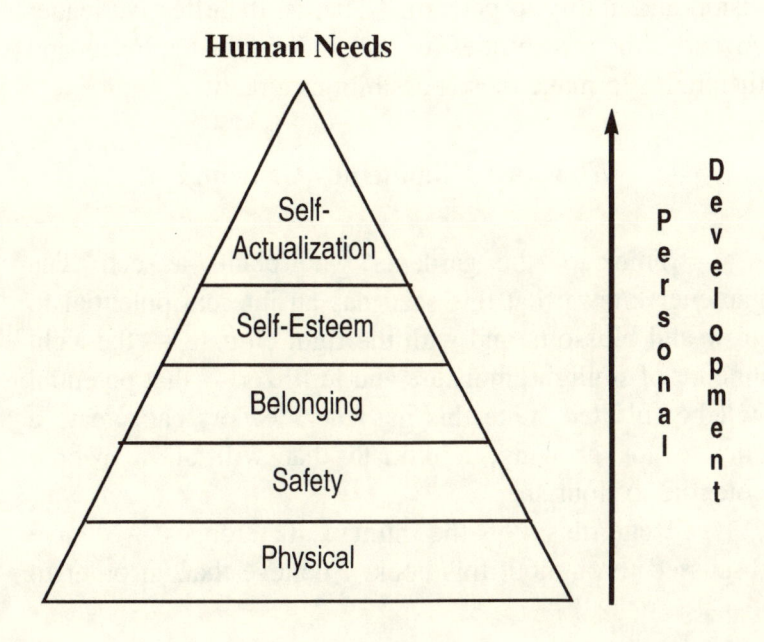

Human Needs

- Self-Actualization
- Self-Esteem
- Belonging
- Safety
- Physical

Personal Development

Self-actualization = Fulfilling our human potential
Self-esteem = Feeling valuable because of who we are, not just what we do
Belonging = Feeling we are important to others
Safety = Knowing that we are not in danger
Physical = Food, clothing, shelter, etc.

This theory suggests that if we can live and work in a climate that meets our first four needs, we will automatically grow to be the best we can be — to be exceptional. In other words, we have an internal drive to blossom into that unique, rare, extraordinary person we were created to be. Not only is this idea personally appealing, but it is also completely consistent with current leadership thinking. As management expert Peter Drucker puts it, "The one contribution a manager is uniquely expected to make is to give vision and ability to perform." That is, the effective leader envisions the possibilities for each individual employee, and then helps to make those possibilities a reality.

What Is A Climate For Growing?

Think of the gardener who plants a seed. The gardener knows that this seed has an internal potential to grow and blossom, and with the right climate — the right amount of sunlight, moisture and fertilizer — that potential will be fulfilled. Like this gardener, leaders can create a climate for growing, a climate that will allow people potential to flourish.

Regardless of the human differences we have discussed throughout this book, I believe that, in order to grow, every person needs: *security, connection, accountability.*

Security means not only being safe from physical harm, but feeling emotionally secure. It means feeling valuable, worthwhile and accepted as a unique individual. Leaders can help their employees feel secure by:
- recognizing talents, strengths and achievements (in culturally appropriate ways);
- encouraging employees to plan and implement a personal development program; and
- using constructive forms of correction that focus on specific behavior.

Connection means having constructive relationships and appropriate interpersonal boundaries. Unlike unhealthy boundaries, which cause people to be either cold and distant or overly accessible (so that self-esteem is totally determined by other people's opinions), healthy boundaries enable people to choose whether or not they will allow themselves to be affected by outside influences. The skills discussed throughout this book, and especially in chapter three, are the keys to developing positive human connections.

Accountability means providing a sense of individual responsibility. When an event happens, people need to separate those aspects of the event that they caused from those aspects that were caused by other people or circumstances outside their control. On the one hand, they should avoid blaming themselves unnecessarily for situations where they could have had little effect, or trying to "fix" problems that are not their responsibility. They should also be able to take action where appropriate and be accountable

for the results of those actions. Leaders can ensure accountability by:
- communicating clear expectations;
- avoiding the temptation to "rescue" employees when people need to learn from the consequences of their actions; and
- providing employees with adequate levels of responsibility, authority and required resources to get the job done.

To see this kind of climate in action, let's look at one last workplace scenario:

Dorothy, a supervisor in a commercial real estate company, is having a conference with David, one of the employees in her group:

Dorothy: "I know you asked me to meet with you because you have some concerns, David, but before we get started I just have to tell you how much I appreciate your conscientiousness on last month's sales summary. Mr. Carruthers told me it was one of the finest pieces of work he's seen from our department — of course I told him that you deserve most of the credit!"

David: "Wow, thanks for telling me that! I can't tell you how much I appreciate that feedback — especially today!"

Dorothy: "Sounds like it's been a rough one."

David: "You can say that again! You know the problem I had getting the listing summary from Helen last month?"

Dorothy: "Yes, I remember how frustrated you were."

David: "Well, it's happening again, but this time it's Phil

— I've been trying all week to get the projections from him, but he hasn't even returned my phone calls! I can't finish that report Chuck wants until I have those figures, and the deadline is Thursday!"

Dorothy: *"I can hear how exasperated you are! It sure is aggravating when things that aren't in your control keep you from doing your job!"*

David: *"Exactly! So what should I do?"*

Dorothy: *"First let's see if I totally understand your problem. You need those figures — and well, you need them now if you're going to cross check them and write the report and have it ready by Thursday."*

David: *"Yes, and I told Phil how urgent this was. I just don't know what else I can do that I haven't already tried."*

Dorothy: *"So it's not as if he doesn't know the importance of getting this to you right away. I'd really prefer not to intercede and call Phil myself — I want him to know that you've got the authority to handle this project yourself. Have you thought of any other ways to get this information?"*

David: *"Well, I guess I could call Phil's assistant, what's her name, Ginny? Maybe she'd have access to the information."*

Dorothy: *"Right! Or, you could call Susan, Phil's boss!"*

David: *"I've got another idea! Why don't I ...."*

Notice that in this situation, Dorothy began by helping David feel more secure. She recognized one of his positive attributes, using a specific stroke (see chapter three.) She also connected with David by encouraging him to openly share his thoughts and feelings about the situation. Finally, she helped him be accountable for the results, resisting the temptation to rescue him and instead assisted him in considering alternative actions that he could take to resolve the problem.

Some Concluding Thoughts

Occasionally, someone will ask me why I am so passionate about diversity. Because of the growing diversity of the American workforce, this country possesses an opportunity shared by few nations on earth. Yes, I believe we should not only value our diversity, but we can go a step further to capitalize on it. Diversity translates into bottom-line benefits, when resources are managed intelligently. But apart from the bottom-line advantages and the obvious benefits for non-traditional employees, I see diversity as an opportunity for healing. It has been estimated that 90% of all the families in this country are dysfunctional. We might question the accuracy of that statistic, but we would probably agree that, even if we grew up in an "ideal family," most of us got the message in school or from the media or at work that it's really not okay to rock the boat, to openly talk about our feelings, to be imperfect or to deviate from the norm. I believe that everyone can benefit from the values on which diversity is based. Whether you are a white man or a physically challenged black woman who speaks limited English, you are a unique human being, and you were created to be an exception — to be exceptional!

Perhaps you realized, earlier in this chapter, that the concepts and skills throughout this book also apply to leadership situations at home. If you are a parent, are you creating a "climate for growing?" Are you letting your children know — loud and clear — that they have your approval to be themselves? (In fact, it's inevitable, but it's okay to let your differentness show!) Even "ordinary people" can be extraordinary when they are given permission to blossom into the special person God created them to be.

Happiness lies in being your best,
Becoming unique, set apart from the rest.
The road is unclear, destination unknown;
Only when you've arrived
You'll know that you've grown.
So choose your path knowing,
With Joy you'll be flowing,
And strive to create
A climate for growing!

Appendix

Bibliography and References

Blank, R. and Slipp, S., *Voices of Diversity,* Amacom, 1994.

Buchholz, S. and Roth, T., *Creating the High-Performance Team,* Wiley, 1987.

Cox, T., Jr., *Cultural Diversity in Organizations,* Berrett-Koehler Publishers, 1993.

Drucker, P. E., *People and Performance,* Harper's College Press, 1977.

Fernandez, J. B., *Managing a Diverse Workforce,* Lexington, 1991.

Fersh, D. and Thomas, P. W., Esq., *Complying With The*

Americans with Disabilities Act, Quorum, 1993.

Gardenswartz, L. and Rowe,, A. *Managing Diversity,* Business One-Irwin, 1993.

Jamieson, D. and O'Mara, J., *Managing Workforce 2000,* Jossey-Bass, 1991.

Loden, M. and Rosener, J. B., *Workforce America,* Business One-Irwin, 1991.

Maslow, A. H., *Motivation and Personality,* Harper and Row, 1970.

Moore, C., *The Mediation Process,* Jossey-Bass, 1991.

Morrison, A., *The New Leaders,* Jossey-Bass, 1992.

Simons, G., *Working Together,* Crisp, 1989.

Simons, G. F. and Weissman, G. D., *Men and Women: Partners at Work,* Crisp, 1990.

Smith, M. A. and Johnson, S. J., Eds., *Valuing Differences in the Workplace,* University of Minnesota and American Society for Training and Development, 1991.

Tannen, D., *You Just Don't Understand: Women and Men in Conversation,* Morrow, 1990.

Thiederman, S., *Bridging Cultural Barriers for Corporate*

Success, Lexington, 1991.

Thiederman, S., *Profiting in America's Multicultural Marketplace,* Lexington, 1991.

Thomas, R. R., *Beyond Race and Gender,* Amacom, 1991.

Wagner, E. J., *Sexual Harassment in the Workplace,* Amacom, 1992.

Walton, S. J., *Cultural Diversity in the Workplace,* Business One-Irwin, 1994.

Video Resources

True Colors, available from MTI Film and Video (1-800-777-2400).

Valuing Diversity (video series), available from Copeland Griggs (415-668-4200).

Bridges: Skills for Managing a Diverse Workforce, available from BNA Communications, Inc. (1-800-233-6067).

Intent versus Impact: Recognizing, Preventing and Resolving Sexual Harassment, available from BNA Communications, Inc. (1-800-233-6067).

A Tale of "O": On Being Different, available from Goodmeasure, Inc., Cambridge, MA.

Other References and Resources

Grote, K., *Diversity Awareness Profile,* available from Pfeiffer, Inc. (1-800-274-4437).

Taggart, W. and Hausladen, B. T., *Personal Style Inventory,* Psychological Assessment Resources, Inc., 1991 (1-800-331-TEST).

Thomas-Killman Conflict Styles, Copyright 1974 Xicom, Inc., Tuxedo NY.

Tingley, J.C., *Genderflex: Adaptive Communication in the Workplace,* in *Managing Diversity Newsletter,* January, 1994, Vol. 3, No. 4.

Core Values

I. INDIVIDUAL WORTH

We will respect each person and treat him as innately valuable (even when his behavior is inappropriate or unacceptable).

II. SELF-EXPRESSION

We will support each person's right to be fully himself and express his uniqueness.

III. EQUALITY

We will treat every employee as equally worthwhile, regardless of his age, race, gender, sexual orientation, creed, physical ability or disability, intelligence, education, social class, cultural heritage or any other form of classification.

IV. PERSONAL POTENTIAL

Since we believe that every human being is a work in progress, we will support each person's innate drive to achieve personal excellence and inner peace.

V. WIN-WIN

We will collaborate to achieve our mutual goals, so that together we will create something that is greater than the sum of our individual contributions.

Sample Role-Play Scenarios For Practicing Problem-Solving

Scenario #1   Mary and Joe are two employees who used to be romantically involved. Since they broke up two weeks ago, Mary is very uncomfortable because she feels that Joe is ignoring her and his attitude is interfering with their ability to work together. She has asked Joe to meet with her to clear the air and re-establish their working relationship.

Scenario #2   Frank and Bill have been assigned to work together on a project. Frank wants to jump right into the project, since the deadline is six weeks away, but Bill insists that they cannot get started until they gather all available information about how similar projects were done in the past and the results. Because of their different approaches, they have now reached a stalemate and for the past week have been avoiding even discussing the project. Bill has asked Frank to meet with him to get the disagreement resolved.

Scenario #3   Betty and Liz have worked together for more than 10 years. They have always been very good friends; their children even play together because they live in the same neighborhood. Recently, they both applied for a promotion to the position of group leader, and Betty got the promotion. Since then, their relationship is strained. Betty has asked Liz to meet with her so they can work out the problem.

Observer Feedback Sheet For Problem-Solving Role-Plays

Circle one number for each item. How well did the listener:

1. Ask open-ended questions that required more than a yes or no answer?
    Excellent   OK   Needs Work
       1   2   3   4   5

2. Maintain eye contact?
    Excellent   OK   Needs Work
       1   2   3   4   5

3. Paraphrase, restating the speaker's message in his or her own words?
    Excellent   OK   Needs Work
       1   2   3   4   5

4. Pick up and reflect the speaker's feelings? (Examples: "You must feel really frustrated about that." "You sound really irritated").
    Excellent   OK   Needs Work
       1   2   3   4   5

5. Summarize the speaker's message every so often?
    Excellent   OK   Needs Work
       1   2   3   4   5

6. Allow silence and pauses to let the speaker gather his or her thoughts?
    Excellent   OK   Needs Work
      1   2   3   4   5

7. Avoid getting defensive, beginning to make suggestions for solving the problem or telling his or her own side of the story?
    Excellent   OK   Needs Work
      1   2   3   4   5

About The Author

Joy Bodzioch holds a Ph.D. in psychology from Texas Woman's University. She is a staff development psychologist, professional speaker and president of The Diversity Advantage, a training and consulting firm with offices in Saratoga, California and Dallas, Texas. Prior to opening the California office in August 1994, Dr. Bodzioch hosted an educational radio series entitled "Diversity Tips for the 90s" for two years. She was a featured expert on an international diversity teleconference sponsored by the International Television Association and the International Association of Business Communicators, and was interviewed on the Business Radio Network. Dr. Bodzioch was named Entrepreneur of the Year for 1993, an award co-sponsored by the Bill J. Priest Institute for Economic Development and the Dallas Chamber of Commerce. She is an active member of the National Speakers Association and the American Society for Training and Development, and for two years she served on the Dallas Bar Association's Multicultural Dispute Resolution Mediation Team. She also presented to the 1993 annual congress of the International Society for Education, Training and Research (SIETAR).

For seven years, Dr. Bodzioch was a Center Mental Health Consultant and Staff Development Coordinator for the Job Corps program. She worked as a staff psychologist at the Texas Scottish Rite Hospital and operated a private practice for nine years specializing in healthy relationships.

With a diverse professional consulting staff, Dr. Bodzioch and The Diversity Advantage have served a variety of public and private sector organizations including the Army and Air Force Exchange Service, Hitachi Semiconductor, Department of Labor, Greater Dallas Chamber of Commerce, Soil Conservation Service, Lederle Laboratories and Lederle-Praxis Biologicals, Heatcraft Corporation, GTE Corporation, Western Area Power Administration, Tarrant County Sheriff's Department, Mesquite Independent School District, Dallas County Probation Officers, The Dallas Society of Certified Public Accountants, International Customer Service Association, Southern Methodist University, Fort Worth Independent School District, American Society for Quality Control, City of Dallas, Hastings Books Music and Video, Four Seasons Resort, Fannie Mae, American Cancer Society, Frito-Lay and Sabre Travel Information Network.

Diversity Workshop Information

Yes, We would like to know more about:
- ❏ Keynote Speech (topic _____)
- ❏ Seminar (topic _____ length ____)
- ❏ Workshop (topic _____ length ____)
- ❏ Cultural diversity audit.

to take place in (city)_____
on _____ 19__.

- ❏ Please call me to discuss the details.
- ❏ Please advise your availability and fee.
- ❏ Contact us regarding an in-depth training program for our people.
- ❏ Please send informational brochures.

Name _____
Title _____
Street Address _____
City _____
State _____ Zip _____
Phone _____
Fax _____

Mail the above form to:
    Joy Bodzioch, Ph. D.
    President
    The Diversity Advantage
    14662A Big Basin Way
    Saratoga, CA 95070-9926
       or call
    1-800-297-7353

To order additional copies of

Catching The Wave of Workforce Diversity

Please send _____ copies at $14.95 for each book, plus $3.50 shipping and handling for the first book, $2 for each additional book in the same order.

Enclosed is my check or money order of $_____
or [ ] Visa   [ ] MasterCard
#_____ Exp. Date ____/____
Signature _____

Name _____
Street Address _____
City _____
State _____ Zip _____
Phone _____

(Advise if recipient and mailing address are different from above.)

For credit card orders call:
1-800-895-7323

or

Return this order form to:

BookPartners
P.O. Box 922
Wilsonville, OR 97070